STRUCTURAL CHANGE AND ECONOMIC DEVELOPMENT

Also by Norman Gemmell

SURVEYS IN DEVELOPMENT ECONOMICS (*editor*)

Structural Change and Economic Development

The Role of the Service Sector

Norman Gemmell

Lecturer in Economics, University of Durham

St. Martin's Press   New York

First published in the United States of America in 1986

Printed in Hong Kong

ISBN 0-312-76669-6

Library of Congress Cataloging-in-Publication Data
Gemmell, Norman.
Structural change and economic development.
Bibliography: p.
Includes index.
1. Service industries—Developing countries.
2. Economic development. I. Title.
HD9989.D44G45   1986   338.4'6'091724   85-24996
ISBN 0-312-76669-6

To Dorothy

Contents

PART IV   RESULTS AND PROSPECTS

Preface

This book examines some aspects of the process of structural change during development and is concerned primarily with the role of service activities in that process. Regrettably, much previous literature on the subject of structural change has ignored, or shown only passing interest in, the service sector. Rather, students of development economics can find much on the transformation of economies from rural, agrarian societies to those dominated by urban, manufacturing structures. They are likely to have to search much harder to find out more about the role of the services, despite the fact that this sector is larger than manufacturing, in terms of employment or GNP, in *many* developed and less developed countries. It is hoped that the research reported in this book will make that search both easier and worthwhile!

One of the purposes of this book is to emphasise the importance of distinguishing between services which are 'marketed', that is, sold through the market mechanism, and those which are 'non-marketed', usually provided by government, either free or at least at prices which are not determined by usual market motivations. Examinations of the causes and consequences of the growth of these two sectors are generally pursued separately here, since it is argued that the relevant issues are often quite different. A second aim of the book is to provide some comparative evidence on service sectors in developing countries, by bringing together case studies of a number of countries, and by examining the Egyptian service sector in some detail.

The research reported here was carried out over several years and special thanks are due to my wife, Dorothy, without whose support and encouragement this book would not have been completed. I am particularly grateful to John Creedy for permission to include material from three jointly-written papers (in Chapters 4 and 5) and for providing valuable comments on several drafts of most chapters. His encouragement has been invaluable. Special thanks are due to Jill Peters for her excellent computing assistance, to Robert Bacon, Walter Eltis and Rodney Wilson for comments on various parts of the book, and to Julie Bushby and Kathryn Cowton who typed the manuscript with their usual efficiency.

I should also like to thank Shell (UK) and especially Alan Peters, for generous financial support of the early stages of this research. Without that support I would not have been able to make two visits to Egypt (in 1977 and 1979) which proved most useful.

Finally, I am grateful to the editors and publishers of the following journals who have kindly permitted me to include material from previously published papers in this book. These are the *Journal of Comparative Economics* and Academic Press; the *Journal of Development Studies* and Frank Cass & Co.; *The Manchester School* and Manchester University Press; *Oxford Economic Papers* and Clarendon Press; *Public Finance* and Stichting Tijdschrift voor Openbare Financien; the *Scottish Journal of Political Economy* and the Scottish Economic Society; and *The Developing Economies* and the Institute of Developing Economies.

Durham NORMAN GEMMELL

Part I
Introduction

1 Concepts and Problems

1.1 INTRODUCTION

Interest in 'structural change' has been fundamental to development economics since the earliest days of the subject. Following the seminal contribution of Lewis (1954) it has become commonplace when modelling the process of development to consider it appropriate to divide an economy into at least two sectors. These have usually taken the form of a rural/agricultural/traditional sector and an urban/industrial/modern sector, where these two sectors have sufficiently different characteristics to warrant distinguishing between them. Recent evidence from developing countries, however, has suggested that, at least for some purposes, a *dual* economy model with traditional and modern sectors, may need to be replaced by a three sector model which can account for significant differences between rural and urban 'traditional' sectors. Recent migration models, for example, such as Fields (1975) and Mazumdar (1973) include an urban 'traditional' sector because the observed processes of labour resource transfers were clearly not adequately depicted by shifts from a rural/agricultural labour force to a modern/industrial labour force. These structural changes are seen as fundamental to the development process. Thus, according to Chenery (1979), 'Economic development can be viewed as a set of interrelated changes in the structure of an economy that are required for its continued growth ... These structural changes define the transformation of a traditional to a modern economic system' (p. xvi).

For developed countries, since the work of Fisher (1933, 1939) and Clark (1940) economic activity has often been divided along structural lines into agricultural, industrial and service sectors (or primary, secondary and tertiary). It has been argued that the roles of these sectors (whose definitions are considered more closely below) change with the level of development or per capita income reached. The recent growth of service sectors in developed countries has generated renewed interest and a great deal of discussion among economists, concerning the role of the service sector in the process of economic growth.

The role of service activities in developing countries however remains a subject which has received relatively little research effort. While the growth in urban traditional or 'informal' activities, many of which could be classed as services, has been studied in recent years, the growth of modern services has generally received little attention. This is perhaps most apparent with reference to publicly-provided services which have been examined and analysed at length in developed countries, but remain largely neglected in developing countries. In particular, knowledge of the causes and consequences of structural change involving public service sectors *during the development process* remains limited, with most previous work being concerned with specific economies at particular stages in their development.

This book aims to fill *some* of these gaps by examining some aspects of the growth of service activities during development. It was readily apparent at the initial stages of this study that the growth of publicly-provided services is an important component of a more general growth in services experienced by many countries. In many important respects publicly-provided and privately-provided services differ from each other such that to understand the processes and consequences of service growth overall it is often necessary to examine these two types of service activity separately. The nature of these differences and their implications for economic analysis will become clearer in subsequent chapters and need not be discussed here. However one important difference between private and public services is that while the former are generally provided through the 'market-place', the latter, in general, are not. The processes determining the production of these two services may therefore be expected to differ. In examining structural change during development this book will therefore consider the respective roles of private and public services.

The study is concerned primarily with three largely separate, though related, aspects of structural change towards service sectors during development. Firstly, it is desired to establish whether there are uniform patterns of structural change for the service sector across countries. Previous evidence has generally supported the existence of uniform patterns across countries for agricultural and industrial sectors, but has offered less support to the view that service sector growth is also similar across countries.

Secondly, evidence of substantial social service growth most of which is publicly-owned and 'non-marketed' (i.e. not sold via the market mechanism) suggests, following the analysis of Bacon and Eltis (1976) and others, that there may be important macroeconomic consequences for the economies concerned. The Bacon and Eltis analysis is extended here to permit examination of the relationship between non-market sector growth and macroeconomic performance.

Thirdly, this book examines some aspects of the growth of tax revenues. When public expenditure increases to provide more non-marketed services, taxation increases may be sought to finance this increased expenditure. It is important therefore to be able to identify the extent to which additional tax revenues may be generated as incomes increase (often referred to as the 'built-in flexibility' of a tax system).

To examine these three areas a number of different approaches are used. Firstly cross-section evidence from a sample of developed and less developed countries is used to identify patterns of structural change towards services and to examine differences between countries in the macroeconomic effects of non-market sector growth. More detailed evidence on the extent and causes of service sector expansion in less developed countries is obtained by bringing together case study evidence from a number of countries in the developing world with an extended case study of the Egyptian economy during 1960–75. Egypt is a particularly interesting country to examine because, as shown in Part 3, it has experienced substantial growth in both private and public service activities. In addition, the macroeconomic changes associated with the growth in Egypt's non-market services appear to be similar to those identified previously in a number of countries by Bacon and Eltis, and others.

In examining changes in tax revenues in the presence of economic growth a number of problems arise. A crucial one is that tax regimes often differ in a number of important respects between developed and less developed countries, and individual countries' tax structures can change substantially over time. A tendency to move away from trade and land taxes and towards other indirect and income taxes, for example, as economies develop, has been noted by a number of studies. Some attempt to incorporate changes in tax regimes during development when examining tax revenue growth was made by Hinrichs (1965, 1966) and by some subsequent studies, but these necessarily involve speculative and stylisted assumptions regarding changes in tax systems over long periods of time. In addition, information on critical tax parameters in less developed countries is often insufficient to permit reliable modelling. It is perhaps for these reasons that most previous studies of tax revenue growth have concentrated on *either* developed *or* less developed countries over relatively short periods of time, and those based on developed countries have generally suffered from fewer methodological criticisms.

The approach taken in this book therefore is to construct a tax model which seeks to identify the revenue properties of a particular type of tax system, as a first step to understanding the development of tax revenues as incomes grow. The model is based on the UK but uses forms of taxation which are fairly typical of developed countries. In addition, since the method of analysis proposed here requires information on relatively few tax parameters, it seems likely that it could be usefully adapted to examine a number of developing country tax regimes.

It is the aim of this book therefore to contribute to two important areas of current research: the growth of services in general in less developed countries; and the growth and financing of public services in particular, in developed countries.

1.2 OUTLINE OF THE BOOK

The book is organised into four parts. In Part 2 the three aspects of structural change towards the service and public sectors discussed in the previous section are considered using international evidence and 'general' models where appropriate.

There are four chapters in Part 2. *Chapter 2* examines patterns of structural change during development, using cross-section evidence, and allowing for the possibility of 'de-industrialisation' in developed countries. Results support the existence of clear patterns of structural change across developed and developing countries for agricultural, industrial *and* service sectors, and it is argued that previous studies may have failed to detect uniform patterns for the service sector because they excluded the possibility of de-industrialisation. In *Chapter 3* market and non-market sectors are introduced and the implications for an economy's macroeconomic performance of differing rates of growth of the non-market sector are examined. By providing a framework within which international comparisons of non-market sector expansion can be made, possible consequences of employment growth in both market and non-market sectors can be considered. Empirical evidence suggests that a number of less developed countries have experienced adverse effects associated with non-market sector expansion.

Chapters 4 and 5 provide models of tax revenue growth. The revenue properties of a progressive income tax are examined in Chapter 4, and in Chapter 5 this is integrated into a tax system including a social insurance tax, value added tax and a system of cash transfers to low income earners. This enables the growth of total tax revenues (within this system) to be identified, allowing for the interdependencies that exist between component taxes in the tax system. It also allows some implications for the growth of non-market sectors to be considered.

Having examined some international evidence in Part 2, the four chapters in Part 3 utilise case study evidence from a number of less developed countries on the extent of, and influences on, service sector growth. As noted earlier, while much has been written in recent years on the growth of services in developed countries, relatively little similar information is available for less developed countries. *Chapter 6* therefore surveys a number of case studies primarily of Asian and Latin American countries. These include both modern (or formal) and informal services, and public and private services in such countries as Israel, Singapore, Philippines, Taiwan, Colombia, Argentina, Brazil and Kenya. Apart from investigations of the informal sector there is a particular paucity of studies on African service sectors. Egypt is not necessarily typical of African economies, but it is hoped that the evidence on Egypt in Chapters 7, 8 and 9 will provide some guidance on service sector growth in an African context.

Chapter 7 examines the evidence on structural change in Egypt and highlights the growth in service activities during 1960–75. This is compared to other countries' recent performance using the methodology/results from Chapters 2 and 3 and to Egypt's earlier historical experience. Possible reasons for relative service sector growth are tested for Egypt in *Chapter 8*, firstly using a simple regression model to identify the roles of incomes elasticities and factor prices, and secondly by a comparison of employment, output and productivity growth rates across sectors. This allows some tentative conclusions on the reasons for Egypt's expansion of service employment over the period. These appear to differ primarily between 'commercial' and 'social' services and between private and public sectors.

Finally, *Chapter 9* applies the market/non-market distinction to Egyptian data for 1960–76 to examine possible consequences of the substantial growth in public services over the period. It is argued that an increasing non-market sector is at least partly to blame for the country's worsening balance of payments, low growth and inflationary pressures, with 'excessive' increases in both defence and non-defence public expenditures identified.

Part 4 summarises the main results in Parts 2 and 3, and draws some general conclusions.

1.3 SOME DEFINITIONS AND METHODOLOGICAL ISSUES

Already in this chapter terms such as 'structural change', 'non-market sector' and 'development', which may have different meanings in different contexts, have been used. They will be used repeatedly in subsequent chapters and it is important that their meanings in the context of this book should be established at an early stage.

1.3.1 Sector definitions

There is a long tradition within economics that an explanation of the growth of various economic aggregates such as output, employment and investment, necessitates an understanding of the composition or structure of these aggregates. Adam Smith, for example, found it useful to distinguish between 'productive' and 'unproductive' labour in an explanation of capital accumulation. These terms were associated with different types of employment, the former being involved in producing 'vendable commodities' while the work of the latter 'perishes in the very instant of its production' (Smith, 1776, reprinted in Skinner, 1970, pp. 430–1). Clearly the relevant structure or components will depend on the aggregate under investigation and what factors are thought to constrain or facilitate the growth of that aggregate. In the case of total production and employment it has often been argued that growth may be constrained by the type of commodities produced and distinctions have been drawn between 'agricultural', 'industrial' and 'service' commodities. Other structures which have been argued to be important however include the destination of goods produced, namely foreign or domestic, the time period over which the goods are consumed, the production ownership structure and the division of sales revenue between wage costs and profits.

The structural divisions with which this study is concerned however are those between agricultural, industrial and service activities. The term 'structural change' as used in this study therefore relates to the processes by which economic resources are transferred from one form of production structure to another such that the proportion of these resources devoted to agricultural, industrial and service production changes.

The criteria used in decomposing economic activity into these three categories have been widely discussed elsewhere and it is not proposed to examine these here. However, fundamental to any division is the view that there is more homogeneity within than between categories which is sufficient to require separate treatment of these categories in economic analysis. Some of the reasons for examination of separate sectors are discussed in subsequent chapters. In discussing these sectors two types of classification are adopted in this book. Firstly, activities are divided into agriculture, industry and services using the International Standard Industrial Classification (ISIC). The detailed allocation is given in Chapter 2; and in Chapter 8 services are compared with a 'goods' sector which includes agricultural and industrial activities.

A second distinction which is drawn is that between 'marketed' goods and services and 'non-marketed' services. (In principle there is no reason why some *goods* should not be included in the non-marketed sector, though in the original definition by Johnston (1975) only services were included.) Once again the reason for this distinction stems from the belief that the processes operating in the 'market' sector are different from those in the 'non-market' sector. For Johnston (1975) the crucial difference between the sectors was that only price movements in marketed outputs were important for inflation. Bacon and Eltis (1976) argued that the distinction was also important because only the market sector could produce the consumption, investment and exportable goods and services necessary for an economy's internal and external equilibrium.

The non-market sector is therefore a subset of the service sector, marketed services being combined with goods production to give a 'market' sector. The non-market sector may also be thought of as a subset of the public sector since almost all non-marketed services are produced and/or distributed under public ownership. The public sector in many countries is of course also involved in the production of marketed goods and services. In this book however the term 'public sector' is generally applied only to that part which is non-marketed. Finally in some chapters the ISIC category 'community, personal and social services' is considered separately (and abbreviated to 'social services'). Most of this group of services in most countries is publicly-owned and non-marketed, though there are likely to be varying degrees of private and marketed services within it. However as indicated in Chapters 2 and 3 *data limitations* sometimes necessitate the use of 'social service' data to approximate the non-market sector and for this reason the terms 'social services' and 'non-market sector' may be used interchangeably.

The term 'development' or 'economic development' is also used extensively throughout the following chapters. There is now a vast literature within economics (and other disciplines) devoted to defining what is meant, and ought to be meant, by 'development'. It is increasingly recognised and advocated that the earlier use of per capita income increases as an index of development must now be supplemented by indices of income distribution, consumption of 'basic' commodities and other social indicators. In this book however the term 'economic development' is used to refer to the growth in per capita incomes. This is not intended to convey any view of development, but rather is used as a summary expression for increases in per capita incomes.

Before turning to an examination of structural change two further methodological issues should be considered – problems of measurement of service sector outputs, and problems of causality associated with the structural change/development relationship and the market/non-market analysis.

1.3.2 Measuring service output

Any analysis of structural change involving service sectors must handle the problem of measuring the outputs of some services. The use of net output or value added to measure the flow of goods and services produced is only reliable for those goods and services which have exchange prices by which they may be valued. Non-marketed services, by definition, have no exchange prices and must therefore be valued by some other measure. For those services, output has usually been measured by non-material input costs – mainly wages and salaries. Thus changes in the 'output' of those services are more accurately to be seen as changes in inputs, making comparisons with marketed outputs difficult. Indeed some would argue that output comparisons of this sort are meaningless or misleading.

In this study the primary concern however is with structural changes in *employment* which can be more readily compared across sectors. Nevertheless, as will be seen in Part 3, explanations of employment growth differences across sectors often rely on output or productivity differences and hence measurement problems persist. The view taken here is that it is preferable to use available service 'output' data despite their difficulties, provided they are treated with caution and used in conjunction with other information on service sector *real* output and productivity.

1.3.3 Causality problems

Causality problems are common within economic relationships where *a priori* reasoning may suggest interdependence among a number of variables. This is true for the structural change/development relationship. Engel's law may be used for example to predict that increases in per capita incomes will cause the composition of an economy's output to change towards industrial, and away from agricultural, goods. Alternatively it has been argued that it is the process of structural change, whereby resources move from low productivity (often agricultural) sectors to high productivity (often industrial) sectors, which generates per capita income increases. Examining *patterns* of structural change in Chapter 2 it is not desired to establish or test for causality in the structural change/development relationship. Rather the objective is to identify the nature and extent of the relationship across countries and over time.

The Bacon and Eltis (1976) analysis has also been criticised on causality grounds. In particular conclusions on the effects of non-market sector growth on the rest of the economy based on accounting identities have been criticised. Since accounting identities do not model economic *behaviour*, clearly they cannot be used to establish behavioural patterns. They may however assist in understanding the processes which affect economic behaviour. Chapter 3 considers these issues in more detail.

Part II
Structural Change, the Non-market Sector and Tax Revenues

2 Patterns of Structural Change and the Growth of Services

2.1 INTRODUCTION

There have been many attempts over the last thirty years or so to identify patterns of structural change during the development process. Most of the early attempts concentrated on the relationship between the agricultural and industrial sectors using cross-section and/or time series data, of which Kuznets (1957) and Chenery (1960) are among the most prominent. In more recent years increasing attention has been devoted to the role of the service sector, and differing methodologies have been adopted to analyse its development path. These methodologies fall into three categories:

(i) Cross-section/time series studies of developed and less developed countries (e.g. Fuchs (1968), Chenery and Taylor (1968), Bhalla (1973), Chenery and Syrquin (1975)).

(ii) Comparisons of sector shares in contemporary LDCs with the earlier economic history of now developed countries, (e.g. Turnham (1971), Berry (1978)).

(iii) Country case studies, such as Bhalla (1970), for Taiwan and Philippines, and Berry (1978), for Colombia.

The 1970s also witnessed increasing documentation of the phenomenon usually referred to as 'de-industrialisation'. This literature, including OECD (1975), Bacon and Eltis (1976), UN-ECE (1977), Blackaby (1978), and Thirlwall (1982), has highlighted the decline in the absolute or relative size of the industrial sector (or parts of it) in many developed countries. A decline in the manufacturing sector's share of employment over the decade has been identified most frequently, though a similar decline in the sector's output share is also confirmed in several countries. This decline is almost always accompanied by a rising share of the service sector, public and/or private, and has created renewed interest, in developed countries, in the sector's economic characteristics.

This chapter will investigate how cross-section studies of structural change can accommodate the recent evidence on 'de-industrialisation' in order to identify uniform patterns of change for the service sector. Alternative functional forms are proposed which, it is argued, provide a better description of recent patterns of structural change than those previously used.

First, in Section 2.2 current approaches to, and evidence on, relationships between the agricultural, industrial and service sectors during the development process are considered. Section 2.3 then investigates alternative functional forms which in Section 2.4 are tested using data from 30 developed and less developed countries in 1960 and 1970. These results allow some observations on the role of the service sector to be made in Section 2.5, and the results are summarised and some conclusions drawn in Section 2.6.

2.2 STRUCTURAL CHANGE DURING DEVELOPMENT

2.2.1 Current Evidence

Testing the relationship between sector shares and per capita income has not always produced consistent results on the role of the service sector. For example, Chenery and Taylor (1968), using cross-section data for 54 countries over the period 1950–63, found strong evidence for a relationship between per capita income and the shares of industry and agriculture in GNP, but little evidence to support a similar relationship for the service sector. They used a relationship of the form

$$\log Y = \alpha_o + \alpha_1 \log X + \alpha_2 (\log X)^2 + \alpha_3 \log N \qquad (2.1)$$

where Y represents the respective sector share in GNP, X is per capita income, and N is population. Similar results were obtained using a semi-log form, by Chenery and Syrquin (1975) and Chenery (1979) who also included a term in $(\log N)^2$ in some regressions.

Using ordinary least squares Chenery and Taylor (1968) obtained insignificant coefficients for the service sector relationships and $\overline{R}^2$s less than 0.4, most of this appearing to be due to the inclusion of $\log N$ in the function. Chenery and Syrquin (1975) found significant coefficients but still obtained $\overline{R}^2$s of less than 0.3.

On the other hand Fuchs (1968) tested the hypothesis

$$Y = \alpha + \beta/X \qquad (2.2)$$

where Y now represents the respective sector shares in employment, and X is per capita income, for 20 OECD countries in 1960. He found highly significant regression coefficients for all three sectors. The evidence of Chenery and Taylor (1968), Fuchs (1968), and Chenery and Syrquin (1975) may be summarised as strongly supporting the following hypotheses, where Y_A and Y_I are the shares of GNP (or employment) in the agricultural and industrial sectors respectively, and X is per capita income:

$$\delta Y_A/\delta X < 0 \quad \delta^2 Y_A/\delta X^2 > 0 \tag{2.3}$$

$$\delta Y_I/\delta X > 0 \quad \delta^2 Y_I/\delta X^2 < 0 \tag{2.4}$$

Fuchs (1968) also found support for the hypothesis that

$$\delta Y_S/\delta X > 0 \quad \delta^2 Y_S/\delta X^2 < 0 \tag{2.5}$$

where Y_S is the share of services in total employment.

The relationships found by Fuchs, which are illustrated in Figure 2.1 (unbroken lines) indicate that agricultural employment falls most rapidly in the early stages of development, giving rise to rapid increases in the shares of industry and services in total employment. However the decline in the share of agriculture slows with increasing development, approaching asymptotically a share of about 3 per cent, while industry and services approach asymptotically, shares of about 57 per cent and 40 per cent respectively. Broadly similar paths were obtained by Chenery and Taylor (1968) and Chenery and Syrquin (1975) using logarithmic forms.

2.2.2 Functional forms

Precise functional forms are rarely dictated by economic theory but it is important that they should not be at variance with the main relevant theoretical postulates, and can at least approximate these within an appropriate range of values. The choice of the above functional forms by Chenery and Taylor, Chenery and Syrquin, and Fuchs, while chosen partly for analytical convenience, can be supported by *a priori* economic reasoning. Development theory suggests, not only that a relative transfer of resources from agricultural to non-agricultural sectors may be expected as per capita income rises, but also (under the assumption of diminishing marginal returns) that the pace of resource transfer will slow as income rises. At low income levels, when the economy is almost entirely agrarian and marginal productivity in agriculture is low, a

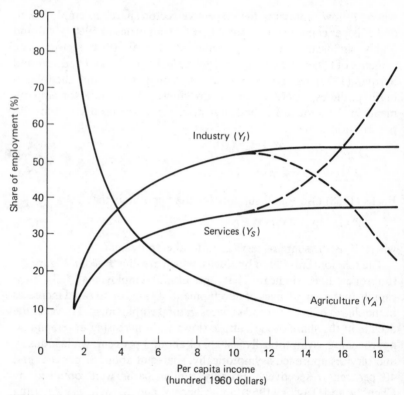

Figure 2.1   Relationships between sector shares and per capita income

Source: Adapted from Gemmell (1982a).

larger decrement in the agricultural labour force is possible for a given increment in productivity, than when the share of the agricultural sector in the total economy is smaller, and marginal productivity higher. Since it has been observed that income and productivity tend to rise together over time, *ceteris paribus*, equal and successive rises in income can be expected to be associated with successively smaller decrements in the resource share of the agricultural sector. Both the logarithmic and reciprocal functional forms can accommodate this.

Economic theory can however also support the evidence of a relative resource transfer from industry to services. It is frequently argued, for example, that service outputs possess higher income elasticities of demand in aggregate, than industrial outputs, so that, *ceteris paribus*, as per capita income rises, industrial outputs will rise faster than service outputs at first, but slower later (assuming the coincidence of higher elasticities with higher income levels). Secondly, there is evidence suggesting that service sector productivity tends to increase more slowly than industrial productivity. Thus, at higher income levels, with agricultural surplus labour all but exhausted, a transfer of labour from the industrial to the service sector will be required even to maintain relative output growth rates between sectors. Baumol (1967) has explicitly modelled this process. Thus it can be argued that the process of structural change for any country can be expected to follow paths similar to those shown by the broken lines in Figure 2.1. The industrial and service employment shares both grow initially at the expense of the agricultural share as income rises, but once the agricultural share becomes fairly small the service sector share begins to expand at the expense of the industrial sector share.

It is clear, in testing for these patterns of structural change that neither the reciprocal functional form used by Fuchs, nor the logarithmic forms preferred by Chenery and Taylor or Chenery and Syrquin, will suffice. The simple form used by Fuchs clearly cannot capture the rise and subsequent decline in the share of industry, nor can it model the sigmoid shape proposed for the service sector. The quadratic log and semi-log forms, while they can account for the declining industrial share, are also unable to model the service sector share. Alternative functional forms are therefore proposed in Section 2.3.

2.3 STRUCTURAL CHANGE AND DE-INDUSTRIALISATION

2.3.1 Alternative functional forms

It was noted in Section 2.2 that the increase in the service sector share at the expense of the industrial sector share tends to occur only when the agricultural share is already very small. Thus, in specifying functional forms for the three sectors, Y_A, Y_I and Y_S, the simple form

$$Y_A = a_1 + b_1/X \qquad (2.6)$$

which Fuchs (1968) found predicted well, may still be used for the agricultural sector.

The most appropriate functional form to approximate Y_S is a cubic in X, whereby

$$Y_S = a_2 + b_2 X + c_2 X^2 + d_2 X^3 \tag{2.7}$$

This will give the sigmoid shape which it is desired to capture in the Y_S function. It might in fact be expected that the service sector share will *eventually* approach some maximum value asymptotically, which cannot be accounted for by a cubic functional form. However, it is likely to provide a suitable approximation over the range of values currently available, and indeed, for some way beyond. In fact, to approximate Y_S a function with a single inflexion point, rather than the maximum and minimum normally associated with cubic functions, is required. This will occur if $a_2 = b_2 = c_2 = 0$, which can be achieved by moving the origin in Figure 2.1 to the point of inflexion in Y_S.

The Y_I function could be specified as a quadratic in X, but this would impose the restrictions that the decline in the industrial sector share exactly mirror its earlier increase and will predetermine the per capita income at which the maximum industrial share occurs. In addition, it is unlikely that specifying all three functions thus would yield values for the three sector shares which meet the required condition

$$Y_A + Y_S + Y_I = 1 \tag{2.8}$$

Y_I is therefore treated as a residual for estimation purposes and specified as,

$$Y_I = 1 - Y_A - Y_S \tag{2.9}$$

Letting the new origin at the inflexion point in Y_S be (f, g), new variables y and x can be created such that,

$$y = Y - g \tag{2.10}$$

$$x = X - f \tag{2.11}$$

and the new functions for y_A, y_I and y_S are given by

$$y_A + g = a_1 + b_1\{1/(x+f)\} \tag{2.12}$$

$$y_S = d_2 x^3 \tag{2.13}$$

$$y_I = 1 - 3g - y_S - y_A \tag{2.14}$$

2.3.2 Inter-sectoral relationships

An alternative method of testing the hypothesis that an increasing service sector share is associated first with an increasing industrial share and then with its decline is to examine inter-sectoral relationships directly, rather than considering sector shares as functions of per capita income. Thus, a direct relationship between y_I and y_S may be examined. The main problem with this approach is of course that both y_I and y_S are endogenous variables and therefore neither is truly 'independent'. However for the purpose of describing how these sectors change relative to each other, either can be used for statistical purposes, as an 'independent' variable, though it is important to stress that this approach provides no basis for discussion of causality between variables.

There are however two reasons why it may be preferable to examine directly inter-sectoral relationships such as these. First, it is suggested that inverse movements in the industrial and service sector shares can be expected once there is a relatively small proportion of the population in agriculture, and therefore little surplus labour remains in the sector. This is likely to occur at higher income levels, but different countries may reach this position at different per capita incomes. Kaldor (1966) and Lewis (1978) have argued that the UK, for example, reached a low share of its population in agriculture at low levels of per capita income compared to other developed countries. Of course, the use of cross-section data to infer patterns of structural change taking place over time must always involve the problem that different countries, while experiencing similar changes, will not necessarily experience them at exactly the same income levels. When testing for the relationships shown in (2.12), (2.13) and (2.14) however, this can lead to substantial horizontal, or near horizontal sections to the y_I and y_S functions, where no statistical relationship would be identified, making the sigmoid shape of the y_S function difficult to identify in particular. By considering a direct relationship between y_I and y_S, which will be first positive, and then negative-sloping (see Figure 2.2B), these horizontal sections will appear as a point, or number of proximate points, making this function more readily identifiable.

Second, there are numerous problems associated with international comparisons of per capita incomes, especially when both developed and less developed countries are included. In many LDCs income estimates are unreliable because of poor collection methods and differing definitions, and their coverage is frequently less comprehensive than in developed countries. In addition, conversion to dollar-equivalents may be inaccurate due to under (or over) valued, and fluctuating exchange rates, though this problem can be partially overcome using procedures developed by Kravis *et al.* (1975, 1978).

A

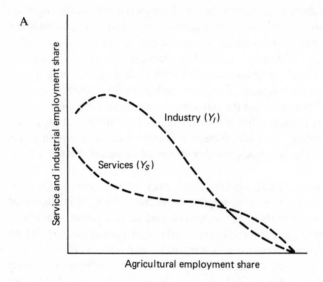

B

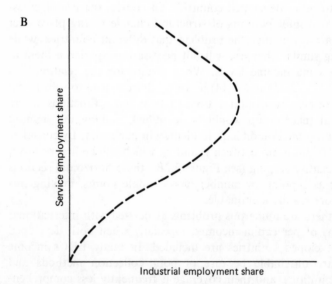

Figures 2.2A and 2.2B   Alternative relationships between agricultural, industrial and service sector employment shares

Source: Gemmell 1982a.

The coverage of demographic data in many LCDs, though also incomplete, is usually more reliable than income data. Therefore it is considered preferable here to examine patterns of structural change using inter-sectoral relationships despite the econometric limitations.

2.3.3 Testing the hypothesis

Equations (2.12), (2.13) and (2.14) may be solved to eliminate x giving relations between Y_A, Y_I and Y_S, such that

$$\begin{bmatrix} y_I \\ y_S \end{bmatrix} = \Pi \begin{bmatrix} 1 \\ z \\ z^2 \\ z^3 \end{bmatrix} + \begin{bmatrix} -Y_A \\ 0 \end{bmatrix} \tag{2.15}$$

where $z = (y_A + \gamma)^{-1}$, $\gamma = (g - a_1)$ and Π is a 2×4 matrix.[1]
Furthermore

$$y_I = \mu_1 + \mu_2 \{ 1/Y_S^{(1/3)} + \delta) \} - Y_S \tag{2.16}$$

where coefficients μ_1 and μ_2 can be determined from the Π matrix, and $\delta = f d_2^{(1/3)}$. These functions suggest that non-linear relationships can be expected between sector shares, possible outcomes of which are illustrated in Figure 2.2.

To identify patterns of structural change allowing for 'de-industrialisation', regressions on equation (2.16) are likely to be most useful. Since the agricultural sector share is already small when inverse movements in the service and industrial sector shares can be expected, it is likely to be difficult to identify de-industrialisation with regressions using y_A as the independent variable. However, if the functional forms proposed in (2.15) and (2.16) are valid, then regressions on (2.15) also ought to provide a suitable description of changes in y_S and y_I relative to y_A.

In testing for these relationships, sectoral definitions slightly different from those discussed above are adopted. In particular, using the International Standard Industrial Classification (ISIC), the service sector is defined to include transport, communications, finance, wholesale and retail trade, and community, social and personal services, while the industrial sector includes only manufacturing. Public utilities, construction, mining and quarrying (including petroleum and gas) are therefore excluded. This avoids the arbitrary classification of those activities which do not fall clearly into any one sector, and allows regression results to be interpreted without considering whether some marginally included sub-sector is biasing the results of the aggregate sector. Previous studies of structural change which have classified all economic activities into three sectors have included public utilities and construction variously in the service or the industrial sector, with mining and quarrying allied either with agriculture or industry. It can be shown (see Gemmell, 1982a) that the effects of excluding these activities on (2.15) and (2.16) is to alter the values of the intercept terms in the first equation of (2.15) and (2.16). Results of ordinary least squares (OLS) regressions on these equations, using a sample of 30 developed and less developed countries in 1960 and 1970, are shown in Table 2.1(A).[2] Before discussing the results, however, some explanation of the sample and the regression methodology is necessary.

2.3.4 Data and methodology

The sample of 30 countries was selected to give roughly equal numbers of developed and less developed countries. This avoids the problem of poor predictions for developed countries arising from estimated regressions based on samples of mainly less developed countries. Secondly, countries with particularly small economically active populations (less than one million) were not included to avoid possible distortions in data on sector shares. Less developed countries with small populations are particularly heterogeneous, with some being geographically small and with small agricultural sectors (e.g. Kuwait), while others may be large, sparsely populated, agrarian societies (e.g. Niger). Unfortunately data are only available on the basis of nation states though this may not be the most economically meaningful classification. In addition, the sample data are based on census returns in years around 1960 and 1970, rather than inter-census projections. Since most such censuses are decennial there are few countries for which comparable data are available after 1970.

The sector shares data require some adjustment before performing the regressions. Since using per capita income as an independent variable has already been rejected, partly because of inaccuracies inherent in such data, its use to estimate g and f (the coordinates of the inflexion point in Y_s) is also prohibited. However for the purpose of performing OLS regressions on (2.15) and (2.16) only g needs to be predetermined. This was achieved by running OLS regressions on (2.16) using an iterative procedure to obtain the value of g which minimised the sum of squared residuals. This yielded a final value of $g = 0.366$ suggesting the turning point in the industry/service relationship from a positive-sloping to a negative-sloping one, occurs with a service sector share around 37 per cent.

Finally, as indicated in Chapter 1, it is interesting to examine separately the development of the social service sub-sector which tends to be publicly-owned, being made up mostly of education, health and public administration services. It can be shown that if the social service sector share, y_{SS}, is approximated by a similar cubic function to that proposed for the aggregate service sector, then inter-sectoral relationships involving y_{SS} can be estimated in the same way as for those involving y_S. With the additional assumption that the points of inflexion in both the y_S and y_{SS} functions occur at the same per capita income level, the value of unity imposed on the coefficient on y_S in (2.16) is unnecessary on the coefficient on y_{SS}. Thus results for both sectors should be similar if the cubic functional forms proposed for both sectors are valid.

2.4 REGRESSION RESULTS

Table 2.1(A) presents regressions on the pooled 1960 and 1970 data for the 30 country sample, while Tables 2.1(B) and 2.1(C) present similar regressions for each year, allowing differences between the two years to be investigated.

In each table, regressions (i), (ii) and (iv) are on equations (2.15) and (2.16) in Section 2.3.3, and regressions (iii) and (v) are for the social service sector. Regressions (vi) to (x) are comparable linear regressions for the inter-sectoral relationships in (i) to (v). These linear forms would be obtained if the reciprocal form $y_i = a + \beta/X$ was assumed for all i sectors, such as Fuchs (1968). Thus it is easily seen how the explanatory power of the proposed functions in (i) to (v) compare with at least one alternative.

Examining regressions (i) to (iii) in Table 2.1(A) reveals that all coefficients have the predicted signs; results from both service sectors in regressions (ii) and (iii) are similar; and both have opposite signs on coefficients to those in regression (i), as predicted.[3] Although the t-statistics suggests that *individually* coefficients are not significantly different from zero at the 5 per cent level, as can frequently occur with polynomial regressions, when considered together, an F-statistic confirms all regressions significant at the 1 per cent level. Comparing $\bar{R}^2$s

Table 2.1(A) Regression results of inter-sectoral relationships

Dependent Variable	Intercept	y_A	y_s	y'_{ss}	$y_s\delta$	$y'_{ss}\lambda$	z	z^2	z^3	$\bar{R}^2$
(i) y_t	14.99 (3.25)	-1.00†					-86.84 (-2.98)	169.01 (2.76)	-112.35 (-2.64)	0.8565*
(ii) y_s	-6.07 (-1.03)						33.30 (0.90)	-64.69 (-0.83)	44.71 (0.82)	0.8784*
(iii) y'_{ss}	-7.63 (-1.64)						50.30 (1.64)	-112.19 (-0.83)	84.82 (1.46)	0.7603*
(iv) y_t	0.1727 (14.27)		-1.00†		-0.2020 (-34.28)					0.7799*
(v) y'_t	0.4957 (6.00)			-0.6767 (-1.78)		-0.5570 (-5.41)				0.6985*
(vi) y_t	-0.1654 (-32.33)	-0.3752 (-17.38)								0.8455*
(vii) y_s	-0.0452 (-7.13)	-0.5283 (-19.74)								0.8760*
(viii) y'_{ss}††	0.0453 (9.64)	-0.2089 (-13.25)								0.7605*
(ix) y_t	-0.1369 (-16.89)		0.5738 (9.60)							0.6237*
(x) y'_t	0.0498 (5.65)			1.2630 (8.10)						0.5404*

Notes to Tables 2.1(A)–(C) on page 28.

Table 2.1(B) Regression results of inter-sectoral relationships, 1960

Dependent Variable	Intercept	y_A	y_s	y'_{ss}	$y_s\delta$	$y'_{ss}\lambda$	z	z^2	z^3	$\bar{R}^2$
(i) y_I	14.71 (2.47)	-1.00†					-84.83 (-2.23)	164.08 (2.03)	-108.25 (-1.91)	0.8780*
(ii) y_S	-1.67 (-0.30)						4.65 (0.13)	-3.06 (-0.04)	0.78 (0.01)	0.9276*
(iii) y'_{SS}	-5.47 (-1.54)						35.31 (1.41)	-77.95 (-1.33)	59.04 (1.30)	0.9160*
(iv) y_I	0.1560 (9.24)		-1.00†		-0.1938 (-26.17)					0.8146*
(v) y'_I	0.3977 (2.76)			0.0778 (0.12)		-0.4105 (-2.40)				0.7764*
(vi) y_I	-0.1595 (-22.57)	0.3994 (-13.65)								0.8647*
(vii) y_S	-0.0584 (-9.42)	-0.5036 (-19.63)								0.9299*
(viii) y'_{ss}††	0.0483 (11.80)	-0.2215 (-17.79)								0.9174*
(ix) y_I	-0.1191 (-10.48)		0.7036 (8.79)							0.7247*
(x) y'_I	0.0511 (5.21)			1.6034 (9.10)						0.7385*

Independent Variables

Table 2.1(C) Regression results of inter-sectoral relationships, 1970

Dependent Variable	Intercept	y_A	y_s	y'_{ss}	$y_s\delta$	$y'_{ss}\lambda$	z	z^2	z^3	$\bar{R}^2$
				Independent Variables						
(i) y_I	13.90 (1.49)	-1.00†					-79.09 (-1.36)	151.30 (1.26)	-99.28 (-1.21)	0.8105*
(ii) y_s	-5.05 (-0.36)						27.72 (0.31)	-54.52 (-0.30)	38.59 (0.31)	0.8084*
(iii) y'_{ss}	-13.47 (-1.06)						91.02 (1.04)	-206.21 (-1.03)	156.63 (1.03)	0.5395*
(iv) y_I	0.1973 (11.24)		-1.00†		-0.2174 (-21.52)					0.7268*
(v) y'_I	0.5174 (4.71)			-0.9646 (-2.02)		-0.5711 (-4.21)				0.5783*
(vi) y_I	0.1700 (-22.06)	-0.3536 (-10.62)								0.8172*
(vii) y_s	-0.0310 (-2.63)	0.5337 (-10.49)								0.8134*
(viii) y'_{ss}††	0.0429 (5.10)	0.1911 (-5.66)								0.5539*
(ix) y_I	-0.1473 (-12.42)		0.4817 (5.21)							0.5628*
(x) y'_I	0.0563 (3.75)			0.8614 (3.30)						0.2838*

Notes to Tables 2.1(A)–2.1(C)

*F-statistic significant at the 1 per cent level.

†Parameters constrained to values of −1.00 as dictated by (2.15) and (2.16).

††Regression of y'_{ss} on y'_A (not y_A).

(1) $y_s\delta = \{1/(y_s^{(1/3)} + \delta)\}$, $y'_{ss}\lambda = \{1/(y'^{(1/3)}_{ss} + \lambda)$, $z = (y_A + \gamma)^{-1}$, $(\delta = 0.90; \lambda = 1.35; \gamma = 2.10)$.

(2) $y = Y - g$, where $g = 0.366$; $y' = Y - g'$ where $g' = 0.153$.

(3) Figures in parentheses are t-values. All regressions are run over 56 observations (1960 = 30, 1970 = 26).

between regressions (i)–(iii) and (vi)–(viii), it is clear that both linear and non-linear forms perform equally well. The $\bar{R}^2$s in comparable regressions are both high, and very close. In regression (ii) for example, an $\bar{R}^2 = 0.878$ compares with $\bar{R}^2 = 0.876$ for the linear regression in (vii). Tables 2.1(B) and 2.1(C) present results for 1960 and 1970 separately, and confirm that the similarity in predictive ability is evident in both years, though the explanatory power of the regressions is noticeably better for 1960 than for 1970. This result confirms that the non-linear function, while not necessary to predict structural patterns involving the agricultural sector, can nevertheless provide as good an explanation as the linear form. Figures 2.3A and B illustrate the similarity in the predictions of these two functions for the service/agriculture and industry/agriculture relationships.

Comparing regressions (iv) and (ix) where y_I is related directly to y_S the improvement in the predictive ability of the non-linear form, from the linear, is considerable. The non-linear regression yields an $\bar{R}^2 = 0.78$, while for the equivalent linear regression, $\bar{R}^2 = 0.62$. A similar improvement is evident in the industry/social service relationships in regressions (v) and (x), the non-linear form giving an $\bar{R}^2 = 0.70$, compared with $\bar{R}^2 = 0.54$ in the linear regression. Again, in all cases, the sign predictions on coefficients are satisfied, and F-statistics are significant at the 1 per cent level. (Comparisons of the alternative functions are illustrated in Figures 2.4A and B.)

Tables 2.1(B) and 2.1(C) confirm that the improvement in $\bar{R}^2$ by choosing the non-linear function, occurs both in 1960 and 1970, despite the fact that fewer observations exist on the negatively sloping portion of the relationship in 1960. The improvement in the $\bar{R}^2$ is however especially evident in 1970; in the industry/social service relationship, for example, the linear form in (x) gives an $\bar{R}^2$ of only 0.28, while an $\bar{R}^2$ of 0.58 is produced by the non-linear regression in (v). However it is also clear that a reduction in the predictive ability of the regressions from 1960 to 1970 occurs in the non-linear as well as in the linear regressions, suggesting that there are other factors affecting the 1970 sector shares, not accounted for by the use of the non-linear form.

Finally, since the regressions in Tables 2.1(A)–(C) have been estimated separately it is necessary to ensure that regressions within each table are mutually compatible, that is, that they satisfy the condition

$$Y_A + Y_I + Y_S + Y_R = 1 \qquad (2.17)$$

where Y_R represents employment in activities not included in the three

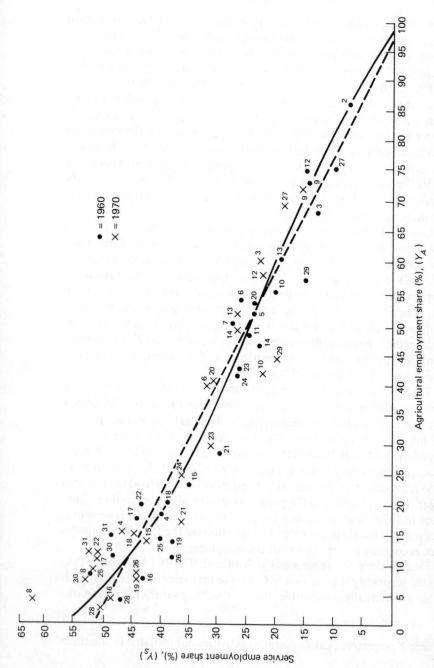

Figure 2.3A Linear and non-linear relationships between the shares of agriculture and services in employment (1960 and 1970)

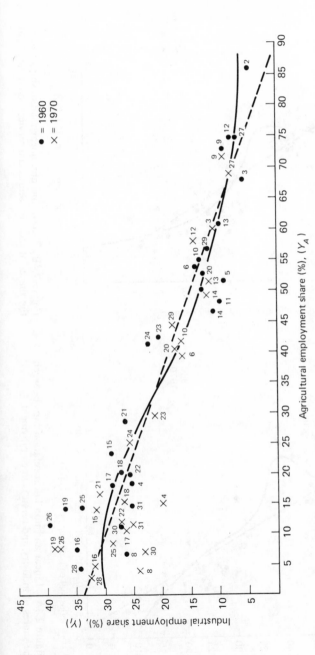

Figure 2.3B Linear and non-linear relationships between the shares of agriculture and industry in employment (1960 and 1970)

Country numbers are identified in Table 2.2

Source: Gemmell (1982a).

32

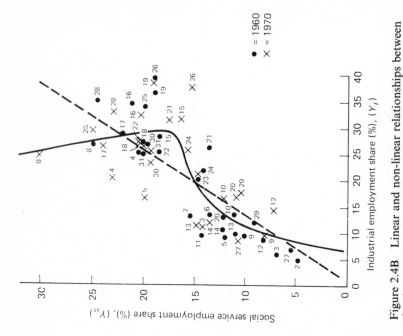

Figure 2.4B Linear and non-linear relationships between the shares of industry and social services in employment

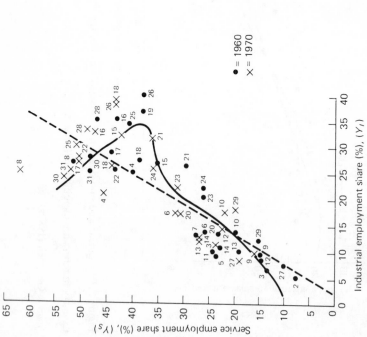

Figure 2.4A Linear and non-linear relationships between the shares of industry and services in employment

main sector definitions. From equation (2.10), since $Y_i = y_i + g$, this is equivalent to testing

$$y_A + y_I + y_S + y_R = 1 - 4g \qquad (2.18)$$

which may be done by estimating $\hat{y}_I$, $\hat{y}_S$ and $\hat{y}_R$, for each observation of y_A, from regressions (i) and (v) in Table 2.1(A). (y_I may also be estimated using regression (iii) in Table 2.1(A)). If the mean of $\hat{y}_A + \hat{y}_I + \hat{y}_S + \hat{y}_R$ is not significantly different from -0.464 (that is, $1-4$ (0.366)), the null hypothesis that the aggregation condition in (2.18) is satisfied by the regressions, may be accepted. Performing such a test does indeed confirm that neither of the estimated means (using the two estimates of $\hat{y}_I$) are significantly different from -0.464 at the 5 per cent level, so supporting acceptance of the null hypothesis, and hence the values of the coefficient estimates. A similar test for the linear regressions in Table 2.1 also indicated acceptance of the null hypothesis.

2.5 THE ROLE OF THE SERVICE SECTOR

The results of Table 2.1 confirm that, although changes in the industrial and service sector shares may not be uniquely associated with per capita income levels, patterns of structural change involving all three sectors can be discerned across countries. It has also been shown that 'de-industrialisation' is a phenomenon which can be incorporated into this method of modelling structural change. Indeed the regression results confirm that the systematic patterns of development of the service sectors in particular will not now be adequately identified using functional forms which have been commonly used in the past. This was found to be especially true of the social service sector where the goodness of fit obtained for non-linear regressions between the industrial employment share, y_I, and the social service employment share, y_{SS}, was a considerable improvement over the linear alternative.

The results invite some interesting general observations on the role of the service sector. Firstly, the service sector share begins to expand at the expense of the industrial sector share at values of about 37 per cent and 34 per cent for the two sector shares respectively, and about 18 per cent for the social service sector. The service sector is therefore already large relative to manufacturing when it begins to expand in association with a contracting manufacturing sector. More relevant than the precise share values at the 'turning point' (which are bound to vary between countries for various domestic reasons), is the extent to which

Table 2.2 Percentage shares of economically active population 1960 and 1970

	Agriculture 1960	Agriculture 1970	Services 1960	Services 1970	Community, Social & Personal Services 1960	Community, Social & Personal Services 1970	Manufacturing 1960	Manufacturing 1970
1. Egypt+	54.0	48.9	28.7	33.0	17.8	19.1	10.0	11.1
2. Sudan 1956	85.8	—	7.3	—	4.6	—	5.0	—
3. Tunisia	68.1	60.1	13.1	23.1	6.4	14.2(*)	6.2	11.2
4. Argentina	17.8	14.8	39.9	46.0	20.6	23.2	25.1	19.7
5. Brazil	51.6	44.3	23.6	35.4	12.1	22.0	8.9	11.0
6. Mexico	54.2	39.5	26.2	31.8	13.5	19.8(†)	13.7	16.7
7. Peru	49.7	40.6	27.3	33.6	15.3	17.5	13.2	12.7
8. USA 1960; 1971	6.5	4.2	51.7	62.5	24.8	30.2	26.5	24.1
9. India 1961; 1971	72.9	72.0	14.5	15.8	8.8	7.8	9.5	9.5
10. Iran, 1956; 1966	54.8	41.8	20.1	22.5	10.8	12.2(*)	13.5	16.7
11. Iraq 1957	47.9	—	24.3	—	14.2	—	9.5	—
12. Pakistan 1961; 1971	75.0	58.0	14.7	22.6	8.1	6.9	8.1	14.3
13. Philippines	60.5	51.4	19.0	26.9	10.7	14.8(*)	9.8	11.4
14. Syria	46.6	49.0	23.1	27.0	12.1	13.3	10.7	11.9
15. Austria 1961; 1971	22.8	13.8	35.1	42.4	18.3	16.5	28.6	31.3
16. Belgium 1961; 1970	7.2	4.5	43.0	48.1	21.4	20.6	34.7	32.0

17. Denmark	17.5	10.6	44.3	50.8	22.1	24.2	28.5	25.9
18. France 1962; 1968	19.8	15.1	38.7	44.5	20.1	20.1	26.9	25.8
19. W. Germany 1961; 1970	13.4	7.5	37.9	44.2	18.9	18.9	36.4	37.9
20. Greece 1961; 1971	53.3	40.6	23.6	30.9	12.1	10.8	13.4	17.1
21. Italy 1961; 1971	28.3	16.4	29.5	36.5	13.5	17.4	26.5	31.2
22. Norway	19.5	11.6	43.6	50.9	18.4	20.3	25.5	26.8
23. Portugal	42.3	29.6	26.2	31.5	14.6	14.4	20.3	21.7
24. Spain	41.3	24.8	26.3	36.4	13.9	15.7	21.9	25.5
25. Sweden	13.8	8.1	40.8	51.4	19.8	24.8	34.2	29.1
26. Switzerland	11.2	7.7	38.2	43.9	19.0	15.4	39.5	37.7
27. Turkey	75.0	68.9	10.2	18.8	5.2	10.6	6.8	8.0
28. UK 1961; 1971	3.8	2.5	46.9	49.4	24.4	22.8	34.8	32.6
29. Yugoslavia 1961; 1971	56.9	44.6	14.9	19.9	8.7	10.6(*)	11.9	17.7
30. Australia 1971	10.9	7.2	47.8	53.3	19.6	18.8	27.0	22.9
31. New Zealand 1971	14.4	11.5	48.5	52.1	20.3	19.4	25.0	25.1

Notes: +Data for Egypt are for 'employment', and have been omitted from all regressions.
*'Services' excluding 'Transport and Communications', 'Finance', 'Retail and Wholesale Trade'. In Yugoslavia, 'Finance' is included.
†Includes 'gas, water, storage and sanitary services'.

Source: ILO, *Yearbook of Labour Statistics*, Geneva, various issues.

sector shares change. It may be noted from Figure 2.4, for example, that as the industrial sector share declines the social service share increases by more than the total service sector, causing a rise in the share of the social component of total services. This accords well with expectations – the 'post industrial' phase of development being associated particularly with increased provision of public welfare services, with fairly high income elasticities. The data also confirm that the de-industrialisation phase is not temporary as is sometimes claimed, arising from slower growth or recession affecting the industrial sector disproportionately. The data here represent the relatively fast growing period up to 1970, and examining changes in individual countries between 1960 and 1970 in Figure 2.4 shows many were experiencing de-industrialisation. In any case, the cross-section data in Table 2.1(B) indicate some de-industrialisation was already present by 1960.

The service sector is of course composed of many different types of service activity. Some services may be expected to decline in importance in association with the industrial decline. In the USA for example, the falling share of manufacturing in employment has been associated with a falling employment share of the 'distribution' sector – a sector largely involved in transportation of industrial goods. Restaurant, hotel and catering services on the other hand may be considered to be less influenced by the manufacturing sector (though backward linkages obviously exist) offering to the consumer an alternative type of expenditure to manufactured goods. In the de-industrialisation stage of development therefore the increasing share of services in aggregate is likely to be accompanied by changing weights of individual services within the total. The previously noted relative increase in social services is an example of a sector with relatively few backward linkages to the manufacturing sector which is therefore relatively unconstrained by declines in the manufacturing sector's employment share.

2.5.1 Predicting structural change

The role of the service sector in *earlier* stages of development is also highlighted by this cross-section evidence, offering general support to previous theoretical predictions. Figures 2.3 and 2.4 indicate that in the early stages, when the agricultural sector is still large, the service sector expands faster than manufacturing. At an intermediate stage (with the manufacturing employment share in excess of about 20 per cent) the reverse is true with manufacturing becoming the fastest growing sector in employment terms. Thereafter services again dominate, changes in the manufacturing share eventually becoming negative. Several authors have pointed to the need of a newly industrialising country to invest in infrastructure facilities including electricity, drainage and transport systems. This has been advocated particularly in the literature on public sector growth during development (e.g. Musgrave (1969), Bird (1971)) since it is common for many of these services to be publicly provided. More recently, migration studies and evidence on the 'informal' sector suggest that various types of small-scale services can be expected to grow rapidly during industrialisation. While the evidence presented here explicitly excludes public utilities, it is likely that it is the expansion of many of the services discussed above in the early stages of development, which is being picked up in the data. Once many of these 'prerequisites' for industrial growth have been provided however the growth of many services, relative to industry, will be curtailed. Whether this applies to the informal service sector remains unclear with little evidence yet on whether significant and sustained industrial development will encourage or discourage this sector. It may be that the growth of informal services, unique to developing countries, will not be suitably represented by cross-section data involving developed countries. Nevertheless the empirical estimates of this model seem to be in agreement with the available theoretical predictions.

It is also interesting to note from Figure 2.4 that a service sector can be expected to emerge before a manufacturing sector (when $Y_I = 0$, $Y_S > 0$), but the reverse is true of the social service sector (when $Y_{SS} = 0$, $Y_I > 0$). Both these observations accord well with the predictions of development theory – a sector providing mainly agricultural services is likely to exist, if limitedly, *before* a country begins to industrialise, but *social* services, frequently financed by governments, are only possible when a country achieves sufficient productivity gains to provide a marketable surplus to pay for these services. This tends to occur in the industrialisation process.

The data in Figure 2.4 (and Table 2.2) confirm the evidence of Berry (1978) and others that Latin American countries have experienced a considerable expansion in their social and total services, most notably Argentina, Brazil, Mexico, and Peru. In the case of Argentina there has been a fall in the industrial sector share as services have grown.

It must be stressed, however, that the functions employed here are not meant to be used to predict at very large values of the service sector share since, as was pointed out earlier, they do not account for a slowing down of the increase in the service sector share which can be expected as it approaches high values. In the absence of observations in that range at present, this chapter has not attempted to construct more complicated functions to incorporate this phenomenon.

Finally it is interesting to apply the functional forms illustrated in Figure 2.2 to the 1960 data used by Fuchs (1968), since Table 2.1(B) suggested that the alternative functional forms proposed also perform better in 1960 than the linear functions. Fuchs hinted that such a pattern might be relevant for the USA but considered that his data supported a different pattern among his 20 OECD country sample, namely the pattern illustrated by the broken lines in Figure 2.1. In fact, had Fuchs applied the functions forms in (2.12), (2.13) and (2.14) to his data he would have found that they fitted equally well, and with the inclusion of the USA in the sample, the data fit better to these functional forms than to the reciprocal forms which Fuchs used.[4]

2.5.2 Changes since 1970

The absence of strictly comparable data for most countries in the sample after 1970, as discussed in Section 2.3.3, makes comparisons with more recent evidence on structural change rather difficult. Nevertheless it is interesting to examine the extent to which the patterns identified in 1960 and 1970 remain representative. Table 2.3 presents some summary statistics on changes in the four sectors in developed and less developed countries between 1970 and 1978.[5] Of the 30 countries in the previous sample there is evidence on sectoral shares in the late 1970s in 26, usually from labour force sample surveys. This source can sometimes suggest markedly different sectoral shares from census data in the same year, so that the data in Table 2.3 must be interpreted with care, and provide only general indications of sector share trends. The table shows the average percentage point change in sector employment shares over the period, for a group of 15 developed countries, and a group of 11 less developed countries. Standard deviations are given in parentheses as one indicator of the degree of similarity of sector share changes across countries.

It can be seen that the decline in the share of agriculture was much greater on average in LDCs, with a mean percentage point change of -8.0 compared to only -2.3 in the developed countries. There was, however, much more diversity among the LDCs. For the manufacturing sector, as expected the LDCs show a rise on average of just over 1 percentage point while the developed countries record a 3.3 percentage

Table 2.3   Percentage changes in sectoral employment shares, 1970–78

	Agriculture	Manufacturing	Services	Social Services
11 Less Developed Countries:				
mean	−8.0	+1.1	+4.8	+3.3
standard deviation	(8.2)	(2.2)	(3.1)	(2.4)
15 Developed Countries:				
mean	−2.3	+3.3	+5.1	+3.9
standard deviation	(1.9)	(2.7)	(3.1)	(2.9)

Note: Of the 30 countries listed in Appendix 2.1, the four omitted here are Argentina, India, Greece and Yugoslavia.

Source: ILO, *Yearbook of Labour Statistics*, Geneva, various issues.

point fall. It is interesting to note that, apart from the agricultural sector the differences among LDCs as measured by the standard deviation, are not very different from developed country differences. The service sector shows a slightly larger rise in the developed countries than in less developed countries (5.1 and 4.8 percentage points respectively), but relative to manufacturing, the service sector share has increased by 8.4 percentage points in the developed countries, as against only 3.7 percentage points in the LDCs. The pattern for social services is again similar to that for total services.

It would seem then that time-series changes in the sample countries after 1970 are broadly in agreement with the earlier cross-section evidence, despite data difficulties. The post-1970 evidence confirms that the agricultural share falls most rapidly in the earlier stages of development; the service share increases sizeably in both groups of countries, but only in the developed countries is this associated with a declining manufacturing share; and social services increase with manufacturing in the LDCs but at the expense of manufacturing in the developed countries. Perhaps the most surprising result of Table 2.3 is that both service sector shares in LDCs appear to be increasing much faster than manufacturing. It may be that this partly reflects the faltering pace of industrialisation in the 1970s in many LDCs, causing employment to increase particularly in service sectors.

2.6 SUMMARY AND CONCLUSIONS

This chapter began by considering alternative methodologies used to examine the role of the service sector in development, and discussed some of the recent evidence on 'de-industrialisation'. Following the cross-section approach Section 2.2 briefly outlined some of the evidence already available on changes in economic structure during the development process, highlighting the work of Fuchs (1968), Chenery and Taylor (1968) and Chenery and Syrquin (1975). It was argued that, in the light of the increasing evidence of de-industrialisation in many developed countries, it was no longer appropriate to use the functional forms used hitherto to estimate structural change from cross-section data, because these would lead to false predictions.

Section 2.3 proposed alternative functional forms which are more in agreement with theoretical predictions, and can allow for the industry/service relationship to be both positively and negatively sloping for different ranges of income. In Section 2.4 it was discovered that the empirical evidence strongly supported these functional forms, in preference to linear alternatives. However, even adopting these functional forms, there was some weakening of the relationships between 1960 and 1970 suggesting that there were factors affecting the relative sector shares not accounted for by these functional forms. Nevertheless strong support was obtained for the view that service sectors expand particularly rapidly relative to industry in the earlier and later stages of development, with substantial similarity across countries.

3 Non-Market Sector Growth

3.1 INTRODUCTION

The relative merits of private versus public production within a mixed economy have always been, and continue to be, an important subject of discussion in economics. Private and public sectors have been analysed and compared in terms of their efficiency, the type and desirability of the goods they produce, and the effects of their ownership structure. In recent years, the inter-relationship between private and public sectors has been of considerable interest both to politicans and economists. Strong arguments have been put forward in favour of a diminishing role for the public sector, and a rise in private production which is alleged to be necessary to combat the macroeconomic ills of inflation, unemployment and slow productivity growth.

Economists have often tried to explain macroeconomic problems using a structural approach involving private and public sectors. Perhaps the best known attempt is Baumol (1967), who developed a model showing that productivity differences between a 'progressive' and a 'non-progressive' sector can cause problems of cost-inflation and slow growth. These two sectors were assumed to consist respectively of, mainly private, manufacturing activities and, mainly public, service activities. More recently Johnston (1975) suggested an alternative division of economic activity could best aid an understanding of inflation. Johnston argued that the distinction between sectors producing 'marketed' outputs and those producing 'non-marketed' outputs was more useful than a private/public division. This distinction was taken up by Bacon and Eltis (1976) who argued that growth in the non-market sector was partly responsible for the UK's slow growth in marketed output, high inflation rates and balance of payments problems. It is with the Bacon and Eltis approach that this chapter is most concerned.

The Bacon and Eltis analysis has now been applied to non-market sector growth in a number of countries, including the USA, Canada and Greece. In each case, it has been argued that expansion of the non-market sector at the expense of the market sector has had some adverse macroeconomic effects. To date, however, there has been no consideration of how these effects may best be compared across countries.

This chapter provides a framework in which international comparisons of the macroeconomic implications of different market and non-market growth rates can be identified. In Section 3.2 market and non-market sectors are defined and the relationship between employment growth and the growth of market sector output is discussed. Section 3.3 then proposes a simple method for making international comparisons, which in Section 3.4 is applied to cross-section data for 27 developed and less developed countries in 1960 and 1970. The results of this investigation are summarised in Section 3.5.

3.2 MARKET AND NON-MARKET SECTORS

The market sector of an economy may be defined following Johnston (1975), as all sectors producing outputs sold 'in the market-place', including agricultural and industrial goods, and services such as banking and insurance. The non-market sector represents those outputs provided 'free' and is therefore usually wholly publicly owned. Alternatively non-marketed outputs may be defined as those outputs for which there is no charge directly related to the amount consumed, such as state-provided education, defence, etc. The definition of the non-market sector therefore closely resembles the Niskanen (1971) definition of bureaus. Niskanen defined bureaus as 'non-profit organisations which are financed, at least in part, by a periodic appropriation or grant' (p. 15). The non-market sector may be considered as *only* that part which is financed in this way.

The relationship between marketed and non-marketed outputs may be easily derived from the familiar national income identity.

$$Y \equiv C + I + G + X - M \tag{3.1}$$

This can be divided into marketed and non-marketed outputs such that

$$Y \equiv Y_m + Y_g \equiv C_m + I_m + G_m + (X - M) + G_g \tag{3.2}$$

that is, total output or income (Y) consists of marketed goods and services (Y_m) plus non-marketed outputs (Y_g). These non-measurable outputs are usually estimated using wages and salaries of public, non-market sector employees. Marketed output is purchased by market sector firms and workers for consumption and investment ($C_m + I_m$), by foreigners in the form of exports and by Public Authorities and their employees, (the non-market sector), (G_m). G_m therefore includes consumption out of wages received by non-market sector employees, transfers, debt interest and direct purchases of final consumption and investment goods by the non-market sector. Public Authorities also use non-marketed outputs measured by the amount of wages and salaries paid to their employees, (G_g).

Thus, since $Y_g \equiv G_g$

$$Y_m \equiv C_m + I_m + G_m + X - M \qquad (3.3)$$

$$\equiv C_m + I_m + G_m + B \qquad (3.4)$$

where B is the current account surplus on the balance of payments. This is similar to the identity used by Bacon and Eltis. However, they define marketed output in terms of final outputs so that

$$O_m \equiv C_m + I_m + C_u + I_u + X \qquad (3.5)$$

where O_m is total final sales of domestically produced goods and services plus final use imports and $C_u + I_u$ is equivalent to G_m in equation (3.3). Using the definitions in equation (3.4) allows marketed output to be estimated using annual data on value added. This avoids the need to extrapolate between years when input-output tables are available to gain annual estimates of final expenditures necessary to estimate equation (3.5). In many less developed countries the accuracy of such tables is in any case extremely dubious.

From (3.4), since G_m includes investment goods (I_u) and consumption goods (C_u), (3.4) may be rewritten as

$$Y_m \equiv C_m + C_u + I + B \qquad (3.6)$$

where $I = I_m + I_u$. Differentiating (3.6) with respect to time and dividing throughout by Y_m, gives

$$\dot{Y}_m = a_t \dot{C}_m + \beta_t \dot{C}_u + \gamma_t \dot{I} + \delta_t \dot{B} \qquad (3.7)$$

where a_t, β_t, γ_t and δ_t represent the respective instantaneous shares of C_m, C_u, I and B in marketed output, Y_m, and where $\dot{Y}_m$, $\dot{C}_m$, $\dot{C}_u$, $\dot{I}$ and $\dot{B}$ represent the rates of change in each of the variables.

In addition it can be shown that the rate of growth of consumption in each sector is equal to the sum of the rates of growth of consumption per employee in each sector, $\dot{c}_m$ and $\dot{c}_u$, and the rates of employment growth in each sector, $\dot{E}_m$ and $\dot{E}_u$. This implies that faster employment growth can only be achieved at the cost of slower growth in consumption per employee, *if* total consumption growth is to remain constant.

Equation (3.7) may therefore be rewritten as (omitting time subscripts)

$$\dot{Y}_m = a(\dot{c}_m + \dot{E}_m) + \beta(\dot{c}_u + \dot{E}_u) + \gamma_I \dot{I} + \delta \dot{B} \qquad (3.8)$$

The growth of marketed output is now expressed as a weighted average of the growth in consumption and employment in both sectors, investment and the balance of payments. Equation (3.8) shows that, *for a given value of* $\dot{Y}_m$, faster employment growth in either sector must reduce the growth in consumption per employee, if $\dot{C}$ is to remain constant. If this does not occur and consumption growth increases, investment and net export growth will be limited. Of course if sector employment growth rates tend to compensate for each other (as for example when, with a constant labour force, reallocation takes place between sectors) this will allow increased growth of consumption per employee in both sectors without raising the overall growth of consumption. The extent of this increase will be dependent on the relative size of employment in both sectors, the size of the labour transfer, and both sectors' propensities to consume.

Notice that (3.8) is an *ex post* equation and does not attempt to identify causality. It is not possible to say *a priori* whether or not a change in one of the variables on the right-hand side of (3.8) will lead to a change in $\dot{Y}_m$ via multiplier effects or to an opposite change in one or more of the remaining right-hand side variables (though on a full employment growth path the latter is more likely). However equation (3.8) does permit *ex post* consideration of the effects on the right-hand side variables of one or more of them growing faster than marketed output. It may be argued, for example, that allowing non-market employment to grow faster than marketed output will have multiplier effects and thus eventually raise marketed output growth. Nevertheless, as long as $\dot{E}_u$ exceeds $\dot{Y}_m$ other variables in (3.8), (which also have associated multiplier effects) will be reduced.

To examine the implications of different employment growth rates in the market and non-market sectors relative to marketed output, it is helpful to arrange equation (3.8) to give

$$\dot{Y}_m - (a\dot{E}_m + \beta\dot{E}_u) = a\dot{c}_m + \beta\dot{c}_u + \gamma\dot{I} + \delta\dot{B} \qquad (3.9)$$

Since $a\dot{E}_m + \beta\dot{E}_u$ is the growth in consumption as a result of employment expansion in either sector, equation (3.9) shows that growth in consumption per employee, investment growth and net export growth are limited in the aggregate to the difference between marketed output growth and the growth in consumption arising from increased employment. Thus countries that experience faster expansion of market and/or non-market employment relative to $\dot{Y}_m$, must also experience reduced consumption growth of marketed output by the existing labour force, and/or investment, and/or a worsening balance of payments.

Equation (3.9) also indicates that in countries experiencing rapid population growth where employment creating policies (in either sector) are often adopted to minimise unemployment, adverse macro-economic consequences will occur if marketed output growth is not simultaneously raised. However, for countries which increase *non-market* employment growth, rather than adopt policies to encourage faster market employment growth, simultaneous and commensurate increases in $\dot{Y}_m$ may be less likely. As Bacon and Eltis (1976) have emphasised, in the short run increases in the growth of market employment can be expected, via the production function relationship, to increase $\dot{Y}_m$ whereas increases in non-market employment growth will only change $\dot{Y}_m$ to the extent of the net multiplier effects. Of course, if non-marketed outputs are inputs to the market sector, expansion of the non-market sector may enable marketed output growth to increase. In some less developed countries where a large proportion of the market sector is publicly controlled, it is tempting for governments to expand market employment beyond that dictated by the production function, so that $\dot{Y}_m$ will not necessarily increase with $\dot{E}_m$.

Finally it has been argued in much of the literature on the choice of criteria for investment allocation, that social welfare functions should include effects on consumption, the balance of payments, and income distribution. Equation (3.9) shows that government decisions about employment in the non-market sector also have important implications for social welfare via the balance of payments and consumption. But even if employment creation enters the social welfare function independently, (3.9) shows the trade-off between employment growth and other variables in the equation.

3.3 CROSS-COUNTRY COMPARISONS

It was shown in equation (3.9) that the difference between the two left-hand side variables, $\dot{Y}_m$ and $(a\dot{E}_m + \beta\dot{E}_u)$ is equal to the sum of the growth in consumption per employee, investment and net exports, all of which are frequent policy goals of governments. It is interesting therefore to assess how this constraint varies for different countries.

This may be done by considering differences in $\dot{Y}_m$ and $(a\dot{E}_m + \beta\dot{E}_u)$ which can be shown diagrammatically, as in Figure 3.1 where $\dot{N} = a\dot{E}_m + \beta\dot{E}_u$.

In quadrant A, OP indicates points of equality between $\dot{Y}_m$ and $\dot{N}$, that is, positive values for any variable on the right-hand side of (3.9) must be balanced by similar negative values among the other right-hand side variables. Clearly the difference between $\dot{Y}_m$ and $\dot{N}$ will be constant along lines parallel to OP, such as RS, and $\dot{Y}_m - \dot{N}$ is greater on lines further from OP in a north-westerly direction. ($\dot{Y}_m - \dot{N}$ will, of

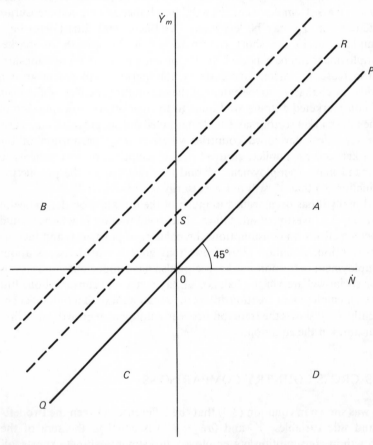

Figure 3.1 Growth in marketed output and market and non-market sector employment

Source: Gemmell (1983)

course, be negative for points below OP). These parallel lines may be referred to as 'isodifferential lines'. Thus countries on the same isodifferential line experience the same overall constraint on the growth of consumption per employee, investment and net exports. For countries seeking to maximise these variables' values, a position on an isodifferential line furthest from OP in a north-westerly direction is to be preferred.

Although most countries may be expected to be in quadrant A, where both variables are positive, observations are also likely in quadrant B. In this quadrant marketed output growth is positive but weighted employment growth, $\dot{N}$, is negative, allowing a larger differential for each value of $\dot{Y}_m$ than in quadrant A. In fact, isodifferential lines in quadrant A can be extended through quadrants B and C, and points above PQ in Figure 3.1 will experience increasing values of $(\dot{Y}_m - \dot{N})$. Observations in quadrants C and D are less likely, at least in the longer term, with marketed output growth negative in both quadrants, and $\dot{N}$ negative in quadrant C.

Finally, it is interesting to compare the growth in marketed output, not only with a weighted rate of growth of total employment, but also with the non-market employment growth component, $\beta\dot{E}_u$, since it has been argued that non-market employment growth in particular can have adverse effects. This can be done in exactly the same manner as that discussed above by considering the differential $\dot{Y}_m - \beta\dot{E}_u$. Larger values of $\dot{Y}_m - \beta\dot{E}_u$ enable growth in consumption per employee, investment, net exports *and* market sector employment to increase. This comparison identifies those countries which have primarily expanded non-market sector employment, relative to marketed output.

3.4 SOME INTERNATIONAL EVIDENCE

In this section the framework outlined in Section 3.3 is applied to evidence from a sample of 27 countries (14 developed and 13 less developed). The purpose of the evidence considered here is to provide a broad indication of various countries' relative positions which can be gained using available data. The sample varies slightly from that used in chapter 2 due to data availability.

Employment and output data, disaggregated into market and non-market sectors are, of course, not readily available. Estimating these categories, therefore, involves two, often conflicting, objectives – maximising accuracy within a country's data and maximising consistency across countries' data. Having defined the market sector, estimating marketed output is not difficult and can be obtained from national accounts using the identity in (3.6). Estimating market and non-market employment is more difficult since even a private/public division is not readily available in many LDCs (though it is usually available in output and expenditure data). In addition, because of substantial public ownership of the market sector in many LDCs, a public/private distinction is often not very useful. Non-market sector employment has, therefore, been estimated from the ISIC classification of 'community, social and personal services', using the same ILO statistics as those discussed in Chapter 2. In most countries these services are substantially publicly-owned and non-marketed, though in most cases a small proportion of these services, such as domestic service, are private and marketed. Possible inaccuracies arising from this classification of the data were examined for some countries where more detailed data are available. This suggested that the results in Table 3.1 are a reasonable approximation. In the USA and UK, for example, using annual growth rates of government and non-government employment (which approximate the market and non-market sectors fairly closely) gave both countries similar relative positions to those shown in Table 3.1. In addition, as will be shown later, the results of this study are in broad agreement with individual country studies which have used more detailed data.

The shares of market and non-market consumption in marketed output, α and β respectively, have been estimated from the shares of public and private consumption in GDP in 1960 for each country, as published in national accounts. Since α and β are instantaneous shares, they should, ideally, be calculated for each year, 1960–70, along with actual annual growth rates. Also since GDP includes non-marketed outputs, this method will slightly underestimate α and β. However, the effect should be similar across countries so that inter-country comparisons will not be significantly affected. Using the data from Table 3.1, Figures 3.2 and 3.3 show the comparisons of $\dot{Y}_m$ with $\dot{N}$ and $\beta \dot{E}_u$ respectively.

Figure 3.2 provides some interesting observations. First, those countries furthest from the origin are predominantly LDCs, suggesting that they have experienced higher rates of marketed output growth and/or market and non-market employment growth over the period, which is what may be expected. It is also clear from Figure 3.2 that this has not necessarily meant larger values of $(\dot{Y}_m - \dot{N})$ in these LDCs. The isodifferential lines indicate that developed and less developed coun-

Table 3.1 Employment and output growth in 27 countries, 1960–1970

| | Average Annual Growth in Economically Active Population and Marketed Output | | | | | |
| | Social Services ($\dot{E}_u$) | Market Sector | | a | β | $(a\dot{E}_m + \beta\dot{E}_u)$ |
		($\dot{E}_m$)	($\dot{Y}_m$)			
1. Egypt+ (a)	4.0	3.1	4.4	0.68	0.18	2.8
2. Tunisia+ (a)	6.1	2.1	6.9	0.64	0.19	2.5
3. Argentina+	3.3	1.5	4.6	0.70	0.09	1.3
4. Brazil+	9.1	1.2	7.6	0.69	0.15	2.2
5. Canada	5.2	2.3	5.8	0.64	0.14	2.2
6. Mexico+	5.0	− 0.1	6.4	0.81	0.05	0.2
7. Peru+	3.1	1.1	5.0	0.68	0.08	1.0
8. USA (1960–71)	3.9	1.7	4.0	0.64	0.18	1.8
9. India+ (b)	− 1.5	− 0.3	3.7	0.44	0.20	− 0.4
10. Iran+	3.6	1.3	8.9	0.70	0.10	1.3
11. Philippines+	7.8	3.4	5.6	0.82	0.09	3.5
12. Syria+	4.3	4.5	5.8	0.74	0.14	3.9
13. Austria (b)	− 1.5	− 0.7	5.1	0.59	0.13	− 0.6
14. Belgium	0.0	0.3	5.0	0.70	0.13	0.2
15. Denmark	1.9	0.6	4.7	0.66	0.13	0.6
16. France	0.8	0.5	6.1	0.65	0.14	0.4
17. W. Germany	0.0	− 0.1	5.0	0.57	0.14	− 0.1
18. Greece+ (b)	− 1.9	− 0.8	8.0	0.75	0.11	− 0.8
19. Italy	3.4	− 0.9	5.9	0.64	0.12	− 0.2
20. Norway	1.3	0.2	4.8	0.58	0.14	0.3
21. Portugal	− 0.2	− 0.8	6.3	0.77	0.11	− 0.6
22. Spain	1.5	0.0	8.3	0.72	0.09	0.1
23. Sweden	2.8	− 0.1	4.0	0.60	0.17	0.4
24. Turkey+	9.5	2.6	5.8	0.75	0.13	3.1
25. UK (a)	2.2	− 0.2	2.9	0.66	0.17	0.2
26. Yugoslavia+ (b)	2.4	0.2	6.6	0.52	0.14	0.4
27. Australia (b)	1.9	2.0	5.7	0.65	0.10	1.5

(a) Employment growth rates
(b) Rates of growth over the period, 1961–71
+ Indicates less developed country. An LDC is defined here as a
   country having 40 per cent or more of its economically active population
   in agriculture in 1960.

Source: Gemmell (1983)

tries are similarly spread, with no obvious tendency for either group to exhibit better or worse performance (in terms of the size of $\dot{Y}_m - \dot{N}$) as a whole.

Secondly, many countries, particularly the more developed, are clustered round the $\dot{Y}_m$ axis (in both quadrants A and B), which arises

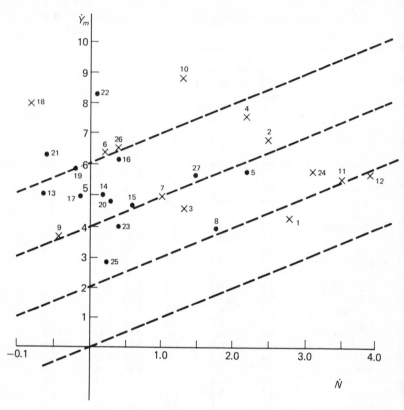

Figure 3.2   Growth in marketed output and market and non-market sector employment in 27 countries (1960–70)

Note: LDCs are plotted using crosses to aid identification.

because a negative weighted rate of growth of market sector employment $(a\dot{E}_m)$ is being counteracted by a positive weighted rate of non-market employment growth, $(\beta\dot{E}_u)$. Thus, in West Germany (number 17 in Table 3.1) and Spain (22), for example, almost none of the fairly high rates of marketed output growth is being taken up in employment growth. The same is true of the UK (25) but with a much lower rate of marketed output growth, and its poor performance relative to other developed countries is evident in Figure 3.2, showing that only the USA (8) in this sample, has a similar differential.

Finally, the worst performers in terms of total marketed output available to increase consumption, investment and the balance of payments position appear to be Egypt (1), Philippines (11), and Syria (12), while Iran (10), Spain (22) and Greece (18) show particularly healthy performances.

The relationship between marketed output growth and consumption growth due to increasing non-market employment ($\beta \dot{E}_u$) is illustrated in Figure 3.3 providing three further points of interest. First, the general pattern that emerges is that different countries' relative positions are broadly similar to those in Figure 3.2. The best and worst performers tend to be the same in both cases.

Secondly, there is a greater relative dispersion of $\beta \dot{E}_u$ values than $\dot{N}$ values, implying that there is greater variability between countries in the consumption growth due to non-market employment expansion. Thus Tunisia (2), Brazil (4) and Turkey (24) have experienced much higher values of $\beta \dot{E}_u$ than the rest of the sample, though high rates of marketed output growth keep them on higher isodifferential lines.

Thirdly, some countries show relative movements between isodifferential lines when compared to Figure 3.2. Sweden (23) for example clearly becomes one of the worst performers when only non-market

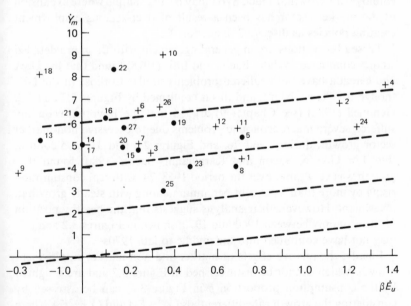

Figure 3.3 Growth in marketed output and non-market employment in 27 countries (1960–70)

Source: Gemmell (1983)

employment is considered and the UK is on the lowest isodifferential line of all countries in the sample. Table 3.1 confirms that both Sweden and the UK have high proportions of marketed output devoted to non-market consumption (particularly when compared to other developed countries) and that in both countries non-market employment grew much faster than market employment. The USA also appears to have a high weighted rate of non-market employment growth relative to marketed output and evidence on the USA by Bacon and Eltis (1978) confirms that America has suffered macroeconomic problems similar to those of the UK. Because many social services in the USA are privately produced the observation in Figure 3.3 may be thought to be biased downwards relative to other countries. Comparing growth rates of government and non-government employment in the USA over this period, however, gives similar results to those obtained in Table 3.1.

Syria (12) shows an interesting movement in the opposite direction to Sweden. Having had one of the lowest $\dot{Y}_m - \dot{N}$ differentials in Figure 3.2, it becomes a fairly typical performer in Figure 3.3. This suggests that the low differential in Figure 3.2 is mainly due to *market* employment growth. In fact, Syria may be an example where expansion of the market sector has been a result of over-zealous employment creating policies as discussed in Section 3.2.

These observations are in general agreement with the more detailed studies conducted to date. Bacon and Eltis (1978) found that the USA and Canada have both suffered problems similar to those of the UK, though to a lesser extent, and this is confirmed by Figures 3.2 and 3.3. Gemmell (1982) (see Chapter 9) argued that the Egyptian economy suffered severe macroeconomic problems due to excessive non-market sector growth, during 1960–76, and Figures 2.3 and 3.3 also confirm this. For Greece, Bacon and Karayiannis-Bacon (1980) found that growth was very rapid over the period 1958–74, with real consumption rising by more than 5 per cent per annum, along with steady growth in investment. However, their analysis suggests that the healthy position of the economy between 1960 and 1970, shown in Figures 3.2 and 3.3, may not have continued into the middle to late 1970s.

Finally, the relative effects of market and non-market employment growth (which cannot be distinguished in Figure 3.2 and are weighted by the consumption proportion β in Figure 3.3) can be assessed by considering the growth rate differentials $(\dot{Y}_m - \dot{E}_m)$ and $(\dot{Y}_m - \dot{E}_u)$. These are shown in Figure 3.4. $(\dot{Y}_m - \dot{E}_m)$ is equivalent to market sector productivity growth (as measured by output per man) so that Figure 3.4 shows the association between market sector productivity growth

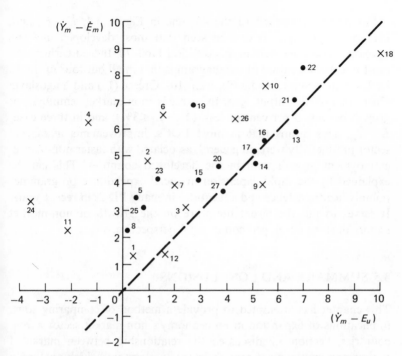

Figure 3.4 Differential growth rates between marketed output and employment in the market and non-market sectors in 27 countries (1960–70)

Source: Gemmell (1983)

and non-market employment growth. Larger values of $(\dot{Y}_m - \dot{E}_m)$, that is, faster market-sector productivity growth, imply faster consumption and investment growth and/or improvement in the balance of payments.

Points furthest from the origin in Figure 3.4 are experiencing fastest market sector productivity growth and slowest non-market employment growth (relative to marketed output growth). Countries identified in Figure 3.2 as exhibiting the healthiest overall performance are evident here – Iran (10), Greece (18), and Spain (22). For points closest to the vertical axis, market sector productivity growth is associated with faster non-market employment growth, so that for countries such as Mexico (6) and Italy (19) the relatively low values of $\dot{Y}_m - \dot{E}_u$ are not as problematic as for countries such as Egypt (1) or Canada (5), because they have simultaneously achieved relatively high rates of productivity growth in the market sector.

For points to the left of the 45° line in Figure 3.4, $\dot{E}_u > \dot{E}_m$ and, perhaps surprisingly, it can be seen that most developed *and* less developed countries were in this position 1960–70. Indeed perhaps the most interesting feature of the diagram is that in all but four of the 13 LDCs in the sample, (India (9), Iran (10), Greece (18) and Yugoslavia (26)), marketed output growth exceeds non-market employment growth by only 3 per cent or less, ($\dot{Y}_m - \dot{E}_u \leqslant 3\%$), and in three cases $\dot{E}_u > \dot{Y}_m$. This means that in most LDCs, improvements in market sector productivity were, in general, associated with faster non-market employment growth than in the developed countries. This can be explained by the rapid expansion in social expenditure programmes (mainly health, defence and education) in many LDCs in recent years. It serves to put the recent literature on the growth of non-market sectors in some developed countries in perspective.

3.5 SUMMARY AND CONCLUSIONS

This chapter has attempted to provide a method of comparing some implications of expansion in an economy's non-market sector across countries. Section 3.2 discussed the relationship between marketed output and employment growth in the two sectors, which enabled a framework to be set up in Section 3.3 allowing simple comparisons of the relationship between increasing market and non-market employment and overall macroeconomic performance to be made across countries. In particular, consequences for the growth of per capita consumption, investment and the balance of payments, can be identified. For countries experiencing slow growth in investment or net exports, for example, this analysis can readily show the extent to which this is associated with expansion of the non-market sector, and how this compares with other countries.

It is not suggested that non-market sector expansion is necessarily harmful. Rather it is intended to emphasise some macroeconomic implications of the non-market sector growing faster than marketed output, so that governments can assess the alternative effects on social welfare. It may be noted, for example, that for governments who consider employment growth as a worthwhile policy goal in its own right, expansion of the non-market sector may have greater adverse repercussions on the growth of other variables, than increasing market sector employment.

Section 3.4 examined the relative positions of a sample of 27 developed and less developed countries, for 1960–70, and found that for countries such as Egypt, Philippines and Syria, the growth of consumption, investment and the balance of payments was severely limited, without similar limits to employment growth, especially in the non-market sector. Of the developed countries, the UK probably experienced the most severe constraints.

4 Economic Growth and Income Tax Revenue

4.1 INTRODUCTION

Examining the growth of the public sector must necessarily involve studying both the growth of public expenditures and the methods of financing those expenditures, of which taxation is frequently an important part. Both of these aspects have been prominent in attempts to understand and explain the changing role of the public sector during economic growth or development. On the expenditure side there is a long history of interest among economists in the growth of public expenditures. The early work of the German political economist Adolf Wagner (1883) continues to generate discussion, while the later contribution of Peacock and Wiseman (1961) has formed the basis of much subsequent research, especially in the UK. The arguments of Bacon and Eltis (1976) concerning the growth of the non-market sector (which forms a part of the public sector) have also been widely discussed. Some developments from their approach were considered in Chapter 3.

On the taxation side most interest has centred round the changing capacity to tax during development and in the composition of the tax structure at different stages of development. Studies such as Martin and Lewis (1956), Williamson (1961), Hinrichs (1965, 1966) and Abizadeh and Wyckoff (1982) have typically used cross-section and/or time series data, often applying regression techniques, to identify changes in, for example, tax ratios as per capita income increases. The concern of this, and the next, chapter is *not* however with the 'appropriate' or 'typical' tax structure at different stages of development but with tax revenue changes for a *given* tax structure. The purpose of these two chapters is to consider how revenue from particular taxes and tax systems can be expected to vary as incomes increase. In this chapter revenue from a progressive income tax is examined, while revenue from a system of direct and indirect taxes is examined in Chapter 5.

The models developed in both chapters use simulated data to examine revenue growth but may be applied to a number of, mainly developed, countries which use similar taxes to those discussed. To enable comparisons with an actual tax system for which certain parameter estimates are available, the models are constructed to approximate the UK tax structure in particular. This need not restrict the wider applicability of the models since many aspects of the UK tax system are widely used, especially within OECD countries.[1]

4.2 BUILT-IN FLEXIBILITY

It is well known that if personal income tax allowances are not indexed to allow for inflation, then a general increase in money incomes will increase tax revenue per person for two reasons. First, it increases taxable income as a proportion of total income for those already paying income tax, and secondly it brings more people into the tax 'net'. The precise extent of this increase, which has become known as the 'built-in flexibility' of the tax, depends of course on the way in which marginal tax rates increase as income increases, and on the distribution of before-tax income.

A variety of methods (often based on regression techniques) have been used to examine the built-in flexibility of several countries' systems. Unfortunately, as Dorrington (1974) notes, these studies typically suffer from two problems: being unable to isolate reliably 'automatic' revenue changes from those induced by discretionary tax changes; and a failure to identify the effects of variables other than income determining tax revenue. In addition previous studies have usually estimated the built-in flexibility of a *particular* tax structure for specific years whereas what is required here is a model which is capable of identifying some of the general properties of a progressive income tax system. The model presented in this chapter does this by giving schedules of total revenue, effective marginal rates and revenue elasticities as income increases.[2] This allows the effects of discretionary changes in the tax system at different average income levels to be isolated. A simple, but extremely flexible, tax function is used which is nevertheless capable of reproducing the essential features of many progressive tax systems in use. This tax schedule is non-linear and is used in conjunction with a lognormal distribution of pre-tax incomes. In addition to being flexible, the model has the advantages of tractability, and of being able to capture the main characteristics of actual systems with few parameters. These properties are particularly important where the model is to be integrated into a wider fiscal model, such as that presented in Chapter 5. Before examining the properties of alternative systems in Section 4.4, the main details of the model are described in Section 4.3.

4.3   A SIMPLE INCOME TAX MODEL

4.3.1   The tax schedule

Consider the following income tax schedule, which uses a single value of 'personal' allowances applied to every individual. This simplifying assumption is not entirely realistic, but it is not difficult to obtain a representative value. Denoting gross income as y, and total income tax as $T(y)$, then in the absence of a negative income tax,

$$
\begin{aligned}
T(y) &= 0 & y &< a_1 \\
&= t(y - a_1) & a_1 &< y < a_2 \\
&= t(a_2 - a_1) + (d - hy^{-k})(y - a_2) & y &> a_2
\end{aligned}
\tag{4.1}
$$

with $h = (d - t)a_2^k$ (4.2)

$k < 1$ (4.3)

A 'standard rate', t, is therefore applied to incomes between the thresholds a_1 and a_2. Thereafter marginal rates increase non-linearly. The condition in (4.2) ensures that the marginal tax rate at the level, a_2, when individuals begin to pay higher marginal rates of income tax, is equal to t. The maximum rate is, of course, equal to d. The condition in (4.3) that $k < 1$ ensures that the tax schedule is progressive, that the marginal tax rate increases as gross income increases, and that the marginal rate exceeds the average rate. An increase in k implies that marginal tax rates increase more rapidly from t (at the threshold income a_2) to their maximum of d. This schedule can also be applied to tax systems which do not use a standard rate, by setting t and a_1 to zero. Equation (4.2) must then be respecified as $h = (d - m)a_2^k$, where m is the marginal tax rate at the level of income where individuals begin to pay tax, a_2. This function is therefore described by only four parameters, d, m, a_2 and k.

The tax schedule specified in (4.1)–(4.3) is extremely flexible and is capable of describing a wide range of profiles of marginal and average tax rates. To give some idea of the extent to which the schedule in (4.1) can approximate the complex schedule actually used in the UK, Figure 4.1 illustrates the situation for the financial year 1977/78. The parameter values used are as follows: $a_1 = 2000$, $a_2 = 8000$, $k = 0.66$, $t = 0.34$ and $d = 0.95$ (whence $h = 229.8$). These values may be compared with the schedules given in Kay and King (1980) for a variety of countries. Notice that it is necessary to use a value of d which is higher than the

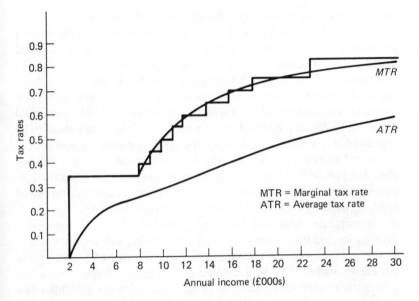

Figure 4.1 Average and marginal tax rates

Source: Creedy and Gemmell (1982)

actual maximum marginal rate (of 0.83), since d is an asymptote and it is necessary to ensure that the profile has a marginal rate of 0.83 at appropriate income levels.

The tax schedule can easily be fitted to any actual schedule of marginal tax rates, using ordinary least squares regression. Over the range $y > a_2$ the marginal rate, from equation (4.1), is given by

$$dT(y)/dy = d - (d - t)[(1 - k)(y/a_2)^{-k} + k(y/a_2)^{-1-k}] \qquad (4.4)$$

For a fixed k (and a_2, which is obtained directly) a regression of the form $z = \alpha + \beta x$, where x is the term in square brackets in (4.4), may be run. Results using different values of k may be compared to find that which gives the best fit.[3]

4.3.2 Income tax revenue and the distribution of income

If the distribution function of before-tax income is denoted by $F(y)$, then total income tax revenue per person, R_t, is given as

$$R_t = \int T(y) dF(y) \qquad (4.5)$$

where integration is over the complete range of incomes $0 < y < \infty$.

When the tax schedule (4.1) to (4.3) is substituted into the general expression (4.5) it can be shown, using the principle of moment distributions, that total income tax revenue per person is a convenient function of just five parameters, d, a_1, a_2, t and k, in addition to those required to describe the moment distributions of the distribution of income.[4] Fortunately the convenient properties of the lognormal distribution $\Lambda(\mu, \sigma^2)$, enable total income tax revenue per person to be expressed in terms of only two additional parameters – μ and σ^2, the mean and variance respectively of the logarithms of income. Values of these tax parameters are available for many tax systems, and although, particularly in developed countries, there is often a variety of threshold levels (depending on personal circumstances) it is not difficult to specify an appropriate value for the single threshold, a_1. The lognormal distribution has been found to describe reasonably well the distribution of the large majority of income earners in a number of countries and parameter values may be estimated fairly readily. Total income tax revenue may therefore be evaluated for alternative tax schedules and assumptions about μ and σ^2.

4.4 PROPERTIES OF ALTERNATIVE SYSTEMS

Having briefly reviewed the analytics of the tax model in the previous section, the built-in flexibility of various tax structures can now be examined. A useful feature of the model is that it can be used to examine the properties of tax parameters for a wide variation in average income. An equal proportionate increase in all incomes will change the mean of the logarithms of income, but will leave relative dispersion unchanged. (In fact, it is not necessary to assume equal proportionate changes, so long as the relative dispersion of incomes remains unchanged.) The effect on total revenue of a general increase in incomes, with an unchanged tax schedule, can therefore be examined by considering variations in μ, with σ^2 unchanged. Comparisons between structures can also be made, in order to consider the implications of discretionary changes at different average income levels. It is most convenient to illustrate the results diagrammatically, which have been obtained using a simple computational method for evaluating the distribution function Λ.

4.4.1 Effective average tax rates

To examine the extent of tax revenue growth it is useful to measure changes in total income tax revenue per person, R_t, expressed as a ratio of average income, $\bar{y}$, which may be called the *effective average rate*. Figure 4.2 shows three examples where it is assumed that σ^2 remains constant at 0.2. This value roughly reflects the dispersion of male earnings over all age groups in the UK. However the results are not very sensitive to changes in the dispersion of pre-tax incomes (as measured by σ^2), over the relevant range of average income. The profile

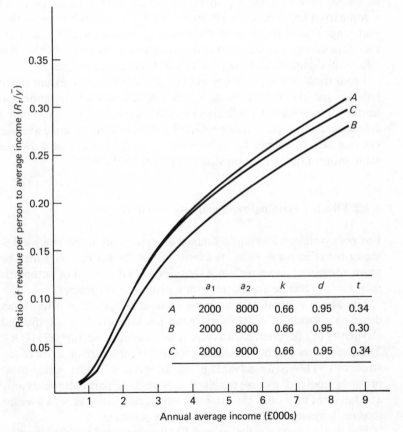

Figure 4.2   Total revenue

Source: Creedy and Gemmell (1982)

marked A in Figure 4.2 corresponds to the tax schedule which is illustrated in Figure 4.1. This profile can be seen to be sigmoid in shape, and asymptotically approaches a maximum rate of 0.95, which is the limiting case where all individuals pay the highest marginal rate. The section of the profile corresponding to low values of $\bar{y}$ relative to the threshold may be thought to be appropriate for a country with a small direct tax base.

Figure 4.2 shows two further profiles. The effects of a reduction in the standard rate t, to 0.30, and an increase in the level of income a_2 at which higher marginal rates become payable, to £9000, are illustrated in profiles B and C respectively. Although all three profiles are sigmoid in shape, they become approximately linear over a range of mean income from approximately £5000 to £9000. This arises because within that range a large proportion of incomes lie between a_1 and a_2 and are therefore subject to a constant marginal tax rate. As $\bar{y}$ rises further this effect will diminish, and the profiles will become more concave.

From these profiles it is not difficult to determine the extent of an inflation tax. An increase in money income due solely to inflation will lead to an increase in the effective average tax rate $(R_t/\bar{y})$ as a result of *a movement along* a particular profile. Constancy in the effective average tax rate can, of course, be maintained by increasing a_1 and a_2 by the same proportion as $\bar{y}$, so moving the profile to the right.

4.4.2 Effective marginal rates and revenue elasticities

For policy-makers seeking to finance an expansion in the non-market sector the effective *marginal* tax rate, and/or the tax elasticity may be more interesting measures, since these indicate the extent of automatic increases in revenue associated with a given rise in incomes.

The above method of examining income tax revenues also allows direct calculation of effective marginal tax rates (EMR), $dR_t/d\bar{y}$, and elasticities of tax revenue with respect to mean income, $(dR_t/d\bar{y})\,(\bar{y}/R_t)$. These measures can be calculated for any tax structure or series of tax structures. This is an advantage of the present model, since most previous studies of income tax elasticities apply to particular years only and have not examined the extent to which elasticities vary as average income increases, using an unchanged tax schedule.

Figure 4.3 shows elasticities and EMRs associated with the profiles in Figure 4.2. As may be expected, elasticities are higher the lower the mean income level, while EMRs rise with mean income. Figure 4.3

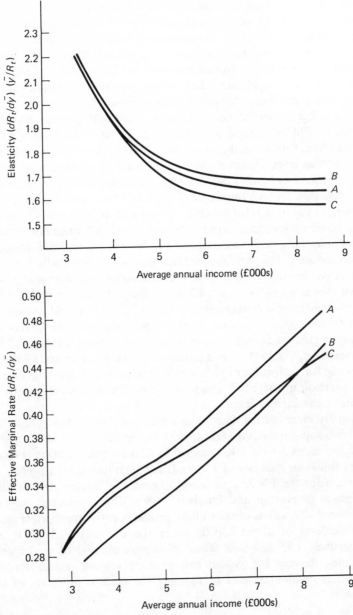

Figure 4.3   Elasticities and effective marginal rates

Source: Creedy and Gemmell (1982)

shows clearly that the revenue elasticity schedule levels out at higher mean income levels, as a consequence of the 'standard rate' section in the tax function. However, the elasticity schedule will decline as mean income rises beyond £9000 (when more incomes become taxable at higher marginal rates). Notice however that in the range of incomes which may be thought currently to be most relevant in most developed countries, the revenue elasticity is almost constant.

The effect of the standard rate on the EMR profiles is rather different. EMRs increase at a declining rate at mean income levels below about £5000. But the increase in EMRs is more uniform as $\bar{y}$ rises beyond this level. However the rate of increase will decline as mean income increases beyond £9000. Excluding a standard rate from the tax schedule changes both the elasticity and EMR schedules. The tendency, evident in Figure 4.3, for the elasticity schedule to level out is removed and the schedules decline more uniformly. The EMR schedules increase at a diminishing rate as mean income increases over the *whole* range of mean incomes. The various schedules are given in Appendix 1.

It is also interesting to note the effects of some parameter changes on elasticities and EMRs. Figure 4.3 shows that reducing the standard tax rate to 0.30 (profile B) increases the revenue elasticities and reduces the EMRs associated with each level of mean income. The effects are however greatest at higher mean incomes. Increasing the value of the parameter a_2 to £9000 (profile C) causes both elasticities and EMRs to decrease for each value of $\bar{y}$. It may also be seen that, unlike profile B, the decrease in the EMR compared to profile A is much greater at higher mean income levels.

Finally, since the tax function in Figure 4.1 (from which profile A is derived) approximates the UK in 1977/78, the results may be compared with estimates for the UK obtained by Hutton and Lambert (1980a). They found an elasticity of 1.78 and, although they do not present an estimate for the EMR, a value of 0.30 may be inferred from earlier estimates in Hutton and Lambert (1980). These estimates may be compared with values obtained from profile A at the appropriate mean income level of about £5000, where the elasticity and EMR are respectively 1.75 and 0.36. Thus this simple method of modelling a complex income tax system can produce sensible values for the measures commonly used to examine the built-in flexibility of tax systems.

4.5 SUMMARY AND CONCLUSIONS

The aim of this chapter has been to provide a method of examining and comparing various progressive income tax structures, in order to assess the effects of growth in incomes on tax revenues. The tax structure is modelled by a simple non-linear schedule which allows for a wide range of variations in marginal tax rates, and the distribution of income is approximated using the lognormal distribution.

Using a simple computational method, schedules for the effective average tax rate, revenue elasticity and effective marginal rate were obtained. It was shown that effective average tax rate schedules are sigmoid in shape, and these schedules allow separation of the effects of discretionary tax changes from built-in changes. The extent to which the revenue elasticity and effective marginal rate vary as mean income varies was examined for a variety of tax structures. It was shown that for each structure the elasticity falls, and the effective marginal rate rises, as mean income increases. However, the rate of change varies considerably across tax structures.

These results clearly indicate that the extent of income tax revenue growth as nominal incomes increase is heavily dependent on the relationship between real and money incomes and the extent of indexation of income tax allowances. It was shown for example that where nominal incomes rise solely because of inflation, an increase in tax revenue results from the 'inflation tax'. Shifting of tax allowances in proportion to inflation will however remove any built-in flexibility. The extent to which tax allowances are adjusted is of course a policy decision which, as has been shown, can substantially affect income tax revenue growth. The consequences of alternative forms of indexation of allowances are examined in Chapter 5 in the context of a wider fiscal model. Further discussion of the implications for income tax revenue growth as incomes grow is therefore postponed to Chapter 5.

5 Economic Growth and Revenue from a Tax/Transfer System

5.1 INTRODUCTION

The analysis of Chapter 4 provided a method of modelling the flexibility of a progressive income tax which, though based on the UK income tax, is likely to be applicable to a fairly wide range of income tax regimes. In order to finance changing levels of expenditure, governments are of course interested in revenue from the tax system as a whole and its flexibility at different levels of income. The purpose of this chapter is therefore to extend the tax model of Chapter 4 to consider the flexibility of various direct and indirect taxes. Since in most tax systems revenues raised by particular taxes are not independent of each other it is necessary to produce a tax model which is capable of taking into account the main interdependencies between individual taxes. It is apparent for example that revenue from consumption taxes cannot be treated separately from personal income tax revenue, since changes in the latter will affect disposable income and hence expenditure.

Most developed countries include in their direct tax systems, a personal and a corporate income tax, and a social insurance 'tax'. Indirect taxes are usually dominated, in terms of revenue, by general consumption taxes such as value added tax, and by various excise duties. As a recent survey by Messere (1983) shows, in the majority of industrialised OECD countries, personal income taxes and social insurance taxes are the most important tax revenue sources, usually accounting for between 50 per cent and 70 per cent of total tax revenue. General and specific consumption taxes typically provide around 10–15 per cent of total tax revenue while corporate and other taxes are relatively unimportant in revenue terms. Of course the specific forms of these taxes can vary considerably across countries with different threshold and rate structures, tax bases and systems for determining liability to tax.

The model proposed in this chapter includes the personal income tax discussed in Chapter 4, a social insurance 'tax' and a value added tax, using specific forms similar to those in the UK system. Commodity-specific taxes, which are used in many countries including the UK, in addition to a general expenditure tax, are not included in the present model. The model could however be extended to include such taxes using information on the distribution of consumption of particular commodities. Corporate taxation is also excluded from the model. The extent to which social insurance taxes finance systems of social welfare (e.g. pensions, sickness benefits) varies across developed countries. In the UK it has often been suggested that the National Insurance scheme is more like a conventional direct tax than insurance contributions towards social welfare benefits. However, regardless of the financing methods for these benefits, their existence affects tax revenues by changing disposable income, income tax liability or patterns of expenditure (with associated effects on expenditure taxes). In the UK, since a fairly extensive system of social welfare payments operates, it is necessary to incorporate this into the model. For this purpose a simplified system of cash transfers to low income earners is used, which nevertheless captures the essential features of the UK system.

Thus, although the forms of taxes and transfers used here are specific to the UK, the model may be modified to reflect the precise forms and interdependencies of similar taxes used in a wide range of mainly developed countries.

As noted in Chapter 4, the growth of tax revenues will, of course, be influenced by the ways in which tax thresholds adjust with changes in nominal and real incomes. It is important therefore, in analysing the built-in flexibility properties of particular taxes, to consider appropriate forms of indexation of tax thresholds. In practice in the UK, the extent of indexation has varied across taxes and benefits, and over time, especially in periods of inflation. However when income tax and National Insurance thresholds and benefit levels have been indexed, it has usually taken some form of price or earnings indexation.

Unfortunately, it is not a straightforward matter to examine the implications of using different methods of indexation in the UK. This difficulty arises because of the complex interdependencies which exist within the system of taxes and transfer payments. For example, the cost to the exchequer of indexing all benefits using an earnings index (when tax thresholds are not fully adjusted) cannot simply be measured by the total value of transfer payments. Many individuals both pay tax *and* receive benefits because of the overlap in the system. Part of the increase in transfer payments is actually met by the higher tax payments of those receiving benefits. The effects of different forms of indexation on tax revenue flexibility are examined in Section 5.3. First, however, the tax/transfer model is described in Section 5.2.

5.2 THE TAX/TRANSFER MODEL

This section describes the main features of the tax and transfer model used, the nature of the interdependencies involved and the resulting constraints on the extent to which the various 'thresholds' may be independently adjusted in response to a growth in incomes. The model is described in more detail in Creedy and Gemmell (1984), where its static characteristics have been examined. Some basic features may first be noted. The model considers only income derived from employment, so that the income relevant for National Insurance contributions is the same as that for income taxation. It is also assumed for convenience that all earnings are obtained by a single member of the household. No attempt has been made to allow for possible labour supply effects of changes in taxes or transfer payments. It must be stressed that the model does not attempt to cover all the fine detail of the very complex UK system, but aims to capture the main characteristics and interdependencies. It therefore provides a reasonable description of *some* aspects of the system, and can identify general flexibility properties, but it is not designed to provide accurate estimates of individual tax flexibility.

5.2.1 Income taxation and National Insurance

The model uses the non-linear tax schedule described in Chapter 4, in which a standard rate of t operates over a range of income from a_1 to a_2, and thereafter has rising marginal rates up to a maximum rate of d.

The schedule of National Insurance contributions in the UK, for those not partially contracted-out of the state pension scheme, can be described as follows. (Contracting out involves further complications which cannot be examined here. The present analysis also ignores employers' contributions and the surcharge.)[1] If $C(y)$ denotes contributions relating to earnings of y, then

$$
\begin{aligned}
C(y) &= 0 & y &< y_L \\
&= cy & y_L &< y < y_U \\
&= cy_U & y_U &< y
\end{aligned}
\tag{5.1}
$$

Contributions are paid when earnings exceed a lower limit, y_L, and are directly proportional to gross earnings up to the upper limit, y_U. The marginal contributions rate is therefore zero above y_U.[2] An important feature of the system is that NI contributions are *not* deducted from income in the calculation of taxable income.

5.2.2 Transfer payments

Since transfer payments are used to finance a significant amount of household expenditure, the transfer system must be specified before revenue from an 'indirect' tax is considered. The system used in the UK is extremely complex and consists of a vast range of largely uncoordinated benefits. However, the basic relationship between gross and net (disposable) income is broadly similar to a 'Minimum Income Guarantee' (MIG) scheme, in which all those with gross income below y_B receive sufficient benefits to raise their net income to a level, b (see, for example, CSO, *Social Trends*, 1983, p. 74).

There are two features of the system which are important for indexation. First, and depending on the relative magnitudes of y_L, a_1 and y_B, some individuals can simultaneously pay income tax and National Insurance contributions, and receive transfer payments. The total amount paid in transfer payments to those below y_B is more than the 'net transfer'; that is, transfers less income tax and NI contributions. In recent years the typical situation has been for $y_B > a_1 > y_L$. Secondly, the values of b and y_B cannot be set independently of the income tax and NI schedules, if it is required to avoid 'steps' or sharp jumps in the relationship between gross and disposable income. These points can be seen using Figure 5.1, which emphasises that part of the relationship applying to lower incomes.

In Figure 5.1 the line marked ABCDE shows the relationship between gross income, y, and income 'after income tax and NI', z. There is, of course, another kink in the schedule after y_U, and it becomes non-linear after $a_2 (a_2 > y_U)$. If $y_B > a_1$ then the value of b must be equal to the vertical distance from y_B to the line segment DE. Thus

$$b = y_B(1 - c - t) + a_1 t \tag{5.2}$$

If b were set at a value greater than the right hand side of equation (5.2), then a small increase in gross income from y_B would result in a reduction in disposable income. Now this kind of situation does occur in practice as an unintended consequence of changes in the system, such

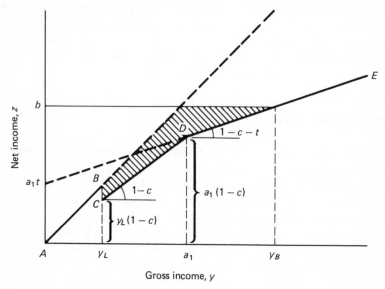

Figure 5.1   Taxes and transfers

Source: Creedy and Gemmell (1985)

as a reduction in a_1 relative to y_B, or an increase in c or t. The shaded area of the Figure, applying to those between y_L and y_B, shows the extent to which individuals both pay income tax and NI *and* receive transfers. In some cases the latter exceeds the former. A time series of the gross value of transfers may therefore give a spurious indication of the extent of transfers to the relatively low paid.

It may be noted that if policy makers take a 'relative' view of poverty, and allow for transfer recipients to share in general productivity growth, then the value of b will be adjusted using an earnings index. Following an 'absolute' view of poverty, however, a price index would be used. Recent policy in the UK suggests a movement to the latter view, although the position has not been stated explicitly. However, from the Second World War until the early 1970s, the real value of benefits almost doubled, keeping roughly in line with average real earnings.

The variable on which indexation policy has concentrated has usually been the MIG, b, (relative to average earnings), but the 'implied' value of y_B (which depends, as shown above, on the nature of the direct tax system) may also be significant for policy. Too high a value of y_B may have adverse incentive effects. An important point to recognise in this context is that indexation of b will not necessarily lead to a similar adjustment of y_B relative to average earnings. From equation (5.2) it can be shown that the percentage change in y_B is a weighted average of the percentage changes in b and a_1. Only where the proportionate changes in a_1 and b are equal is there no divergence between the proportionate changes in b and y_B. However, if b rises relative to a_1 the ratio of y_B to average income rises faster (declines slower) than the ratio of b to average income.

5.2.3 Value added tax

Value added tax (VAT) is the only expenditure tax considered in the model. It is assumed that all disposable income is spent, thereby avoiding the difficulties of the tax treatment of savings. Thus it is necessary only to specify a relationship between expenditure and the amount of VAT paid. In the UK many goods and services do not attract VAT, and the proportion of expenditure devoted to zero-rated goods varies as expenditure varies.

Let q denote nominal expenditure, $V(q)$ the VAT paid, v the VAT rate, and $r(q)$ the proportion of expenditure on zero-rated goods. Then since VAT is levied on the tax-exclusive price of goods and services the relationship between $V(q)$ and q is given by

$$V(q) = q\{1 - r(q)\}\{v/1 + v)\} \tag{5.3}$$

It is therefore required to specify a functional form for the relationship between $r(q)$ and q. Using Family Expenditure Survey data it was found that the following equation describes the relationship very well. (Results are reported in Appendix 2.)

$$r(q) = aq^{-\beta} \tag{5.4}$$

There are no explicit thresholds in the value added tax and therefore the appropriate indexation of VAT is not a policy variable. However, since VAT revenue is partly determined by individuals' allocation of expenditure between VAT-rated and non-VAT-rated goods, it is important to examine whether or not there are changes in this allocation over time. That is, although it has been observed in *cross-section* that a greater proportion of expenditure is devoted to VAT-rated goods by those with higher incomes, the question arises of whether the relationships holds as all incomes rise *over time*.

In order to examine this issue, OLS regressions of equation (5.4) were carried out on the Family Expenditure Survey data for four years (1973, 1975, 1979, 1980). This period witnessed a sizeable rise in nominal incomes and allowed changes in the short and longer term to be observed. The results, presented more fully in the Appendix, suggested two convenient properties for the modelling of VAT. First, the elasticity of $r(q)$ in response to changes in q showed considerable stability; the estimated value of β was constant, at about 0.34, over the four years. Secondly, although α increased over time, the value of $r(q)$ at mean expenditure remained constant, at about 0.45. This suggests that with a general increase in nominal expenditure, the proportion of expenditure on VAT-rated goods remains fairly constant. In modelling the system it would therefore seem most appropriate to adjust the $r(q)$ relationship such that there is no built-in flexibility caused by a changing allocation of expenditure with a general increase in incomes.[3] Thus if $\bar{q}$ is average expenditure (depending on earnings growth and the system of direct taxes and transfers), then from equation (5.4), α in each time period is given by

$$a = r(\bar{q})\ \bar{q}^{\beta} = 0.45\ \bar{q}^{0.34} \tag{5.5}$$

The flexibility of VAT revenue depends on a number of factors in addition to the $r(q)$ relationship. First, the form of indexation of income tax and NI changes the relationship between gross and net income and thus has differing effects on the VAT tax base. For example, if earnings rise faster than prices, price indexation of income tax thresholds reduces net income relative to gross income, as incomes increase. This 'income effect' reduces VAT revenue relative to average earnings.

Secondly, VAT revenue depends on the way in which the guaranteed minimum income, b, is adjusted and, through income tax and NI, on changes in y_B (from the relationship in equation (5.2) above). Increases in y_B, relative to average income, increase the proportion of the population eligible for transfers. This may be called the 'redistribution effect', but it will depend on how the transfer system operates. Various forces will be in operation here. An increase in b which increases the equality of disposable income, by transferring income mainly from those with high incomes to those with low incomes, will increase the proportion of total expenditure on non-VAT-rated goods; hence it will reduce VAT revenue. Furthermore, indexation of benefits also creates an 'income effect', by increasing the disposable income of those in receipt of transfers, which tends to increase VAT revenue.

5.2.4 The complete model

It is useful to illustrate the different components of the model, as shown in Figure 5.2, for a particular set of rates and thresholds. The following values are used: the tax thresholds a_1 and a_2 are £2000 and £8000 respectively; the NI lower and upper earnings limits are £700 and £5000 respectively; and a guaranteed minimum income of £1832 is received by individuals with a gross income below £2250; the standard tax rate is 0.32; and the NI contribution rate is 0.15. These values are representative of the UK system in 1978, although they are rounded for convenience.[4]

Quadrant A of Figure 5.2 shows the relationship between the sum of income tax and National Insurance contributions, and gross income. The relationship consists of five sections. An individual with gross income below £700 pays no income tax or National Insurance. Thereafter contributions are paid at the constant rate c until the £2000 income tax threshold is reached, where the rate is $t+c$ up to £5000. There is a further linear section between the upper earnings limits and £8000 (a_2). Above this level the non-linear section of the income tax schedule applies.

The resulting relationship between gross income, y, and $y - T(y) - C(y)$ is illustrated in quadrant B. This quadrant also shows the effects of a transfer system in which all those with a gross income less than £2250 receive benefits (after paying tax and NI) which raises their net income to £1832.

Quadrant C then shows the relationship between disposable income (expenditure) and VAT payments, from equation 5.5. Finally, quadrant D illustrates the relative magnitudes of direct taxes (income tax and NI) and indirect taxes (VAT), showing the extent to which the former is relatively more important than the latter at high income levels.

5.3 BUILT-IN FLEXIBILITY

This section examines the quantitative importance of changes in tax revenues when there is general growth in real incomes.

The basic framework described in the previous section contains five thresholds which can be adjusted independently. There are two, a_1 and a_2, relating to the income tax schedule; two, y_L and y_U, relating to NI

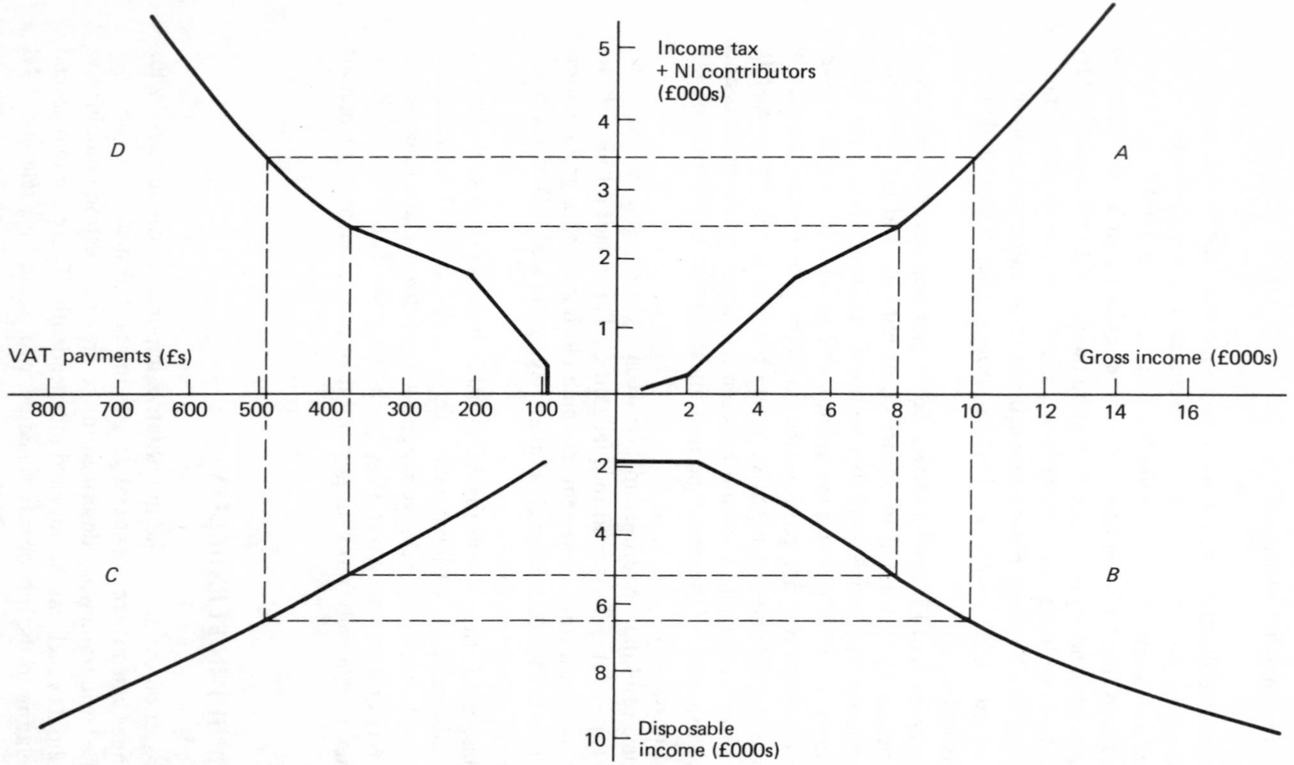

Figure 5.2 The tax model

Source: Creedy and Gemmell (1984)

contributions; and either b or y_B in the system of income support. The policy choices available include widening or narrowing the band of income over which a 'standard rate' of income tax is applied; that is, adjusting a_1 and a_2 using different indices. Similarly, the ratio of y_U to y_L could be increased. In order to focus on the implications of using alternative methods of indexation, this chapter considers only policies which adjust each of the tax thresholds and each of the NI thresholds in the same way, though one set may be adjusted using an earnings index and the other using a price index. Alternative approaches may, of course, be used; for example, the constraint that the marginal 'tax and transfer' rate must not exceed 100 per cent may be used to impose constraints on the variations in a_1, t and c, but these are not considered here.

With the above framework it is not possible to obtain convenient analytical results for total tax revenue. In order to examine the effects on built-in flexibility of variations in the parameters of the model it is therefore necessary to use a simulated distribution of income in association with the tax functions described above.[5] The distribution has a constant coefficient of variation of 0.482, which is appropriate for the UK. The dispersion of gross annual earnings remains constant as each individual's earnings are increased by the same proportion. Growth in nominal incomes is examined by adjusting y_i such that $y_{i,t} = y_{i,t-1}(1+\delta)$, where δ is the annual rate of growth of all incomes. Real incomes adjust annually by $(1+\delta-\psi)$ where ψ is the annual rate of price change. The main calculations use a 2 per cent real earnings growth, based on annual rates of price and earnings increase of 5 per cent and 7 per cent respectively. It is clear that different forms of indexation cannot be pursued for very long, since the thresholds become considerably out of line with earnings. Thus attention is concentrated on the built-in flexibility of the system in the region of a 'base' year, which has a mean income of £3276. Calculations were therefore made for 5 years before, and 14 years after the 'base' year, giving a range of mean income of about £2500 to £8500. The tresholds were adjusted simultaneously with incomes, although some form of lagged adjustment could be examined.

The thresholds chosen for the base year are as follows: $a_1 = 2000$, $a_2 = 8000$, $y_L = 700$ and $y_U = 5000$. The tax *rates* used throughout were: $c = 0.15$, $v = 0.15$, $t = 0.30$ (with $d = 0.95$ and $k = 0.66$ – the values estimated in Chapter 4). The characteristics of revenue flexibility are relatively unaffected by the rate structure, although absolute values of revenue are obviously affected. The calculations use a constant population, providing a basis for comparison (since other changes may result from demographic changes).

As in Chapter 4, the method of examining flexibility here is to consider changes in *effective average rates* of taxation. The effective average rate (EAR) is defined as tax revenue per person, expressed as a ratio of average nominal income, $\bar{y}$. Net revenue per person, R, is equal to the sum of revenue per person from income taxation, NI contributions and VAT (R_t, R_c and R_v respectively), less transfers per person, T. The overall EAR is then simply equal to $R/\bar{y}$. Effective marginal rates and tax elasticities may also be obtained readily using the model, but are not reported here.

Results are presented in this section as follows. First, the built-in flexibility of the complete tax/transfer system with *no* indexation of thresholds is examined. Results are then presented for transfers and each tax separately using either price or earnings indexation. Finally the effects on net revenue are presented.

5.3.1 No indexation of thresholds

Figure 5.3 shows the effective average rates (EARs) for each tax and transfer when there is no indexation of thresholds. The left hand vertical axis refers to values of $R_t/\bar{y}$, $R_c/\bar{y}$, $R_v/\bar{y}$ and $T/\bar{y}$, while the right hand axis refers only to net revenue, $R/\bar{y}$. It can be seen that the largest increase in EARs occurs with the income tax, which may be expected from its relatively high degree of progressivity. The ratio $R_c/\bar{y}$ declines, reflecting the slight regressivity of NI. The decline in the effective average rate of VAT occurs because of the decrease in disposable income, and therefore its decline lessens as the effective *marginal* rates of other taxes decrease. The marginal rates are, of course, reflected in the *slopes* of the EAR schedules. Thus the built-in flexibility of VAT is dominated by the effects of changes in disposable income.

In the absence of indexation the value of the effective average transfer, $T/\bar{y}$, declines at a diminishing rate. In the most relevant range of average income, between £2500 and £4000, it is interesting that $T/\bar{y}$ is falling fairly rapidly – from around 0.12 at £2500 to only 0.04 by £3500. The overall effect is to create a net revenue profile, $R/\bar{y}$, which is broadly similar to that for income tax revenue. However the declining value of benefits serves to raise $R/\bar{y}$ particularly rapidly at lower average incomes.

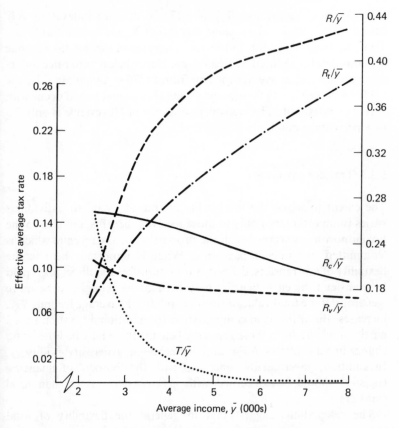

Figure 5.3   Effective average rates of tax (all thresholds fixed)

Source: Creedy and Gemmell (1985)

5.3.2 Income tax and NI revenue

It was noted above that the built-in flexibility of NI was much less than that of income tax. However, when using indexation to either prices or earnings, both taxes exhibit similar patterns. Either form of indexation drastically reduces the flexibility of both taxes. Calculations (not shown diagrammatically), showed that for 2 per cent real earnings growth the value of $R_t/\bar{y}$ of 0.125 in the base year (when $\bar{y} = £3276$) changes very differently within 5 years (when $\bar{y} = £4600$) according to the indexation used. Without indexation $R_t/\bar{y}$ is 0.175; with price indexation $R_t/\bar{y}$ becomes 0.14; while the earnings indexation $R_t/\bar{y}$ is constant at 0.125. Thus the possibilities for 'automatic' increases in income tax revenue are considerably reduced by indexation. Nevertheless with price indexation an increase in average income from £3276 to £4600 can raise the EAR of income tax $1\frac{1}{2}$ percentage points above what would occur with earnings indexation. The equivalent decrease in NI revenue is only 0.3 of a percentage point.

5.3.3 Transfer payments

The extent to which the total value of transfers paid to individuals varies is important, not only to those receiving benefits, but also to the tax authorities concerned with the proportion of tax revenue which is 'committed' to transfer payments. What is important here is the flexibility of *net* transfers, defined as total transfers less direct taxes paid by transfer recipients. Benefits may perhaps be thought to be more 'generous' if the total value of transfers relative to average income, $T/\bar{y}$, increases. But if this is in compensation for additional taxation raised partly or wholly from those receiving benefits there may be little or no change in net transfers, $NT/\bar{y}$, and the increased 'generosity' is illusory. In addition, governments concerned with the 'burden' of financing transfers should be concerned with *net* transfers rather than total transfers.

The calculations suggest that in general the flexibility of total transfers is sensitive to the form of indexation of b, but is not sensitive to the form of indexation of NI or income tax thresholds. Some examples are shown in Figure 5.4. With b, a_1 and a_2 all linked to prices, as in profile A, transfers decrease relative to average income, such that $T/\bar{y}$ falls from about 0.06 to 0.04 as $\bar{y}$ increases from about £2500 to £3500. Net transfers, $NT/\bar{y}$, similarly fall about $1\frac{1}{2}$ percentage points, as shown in profile A'. The 'dash', as in A', indicates that the profile relates to net transfers, using the same indexation method as in profile A. Changing the indexation of income tax so that thresholds adjust with earnings, as in profile C, has only a slight effect on the flexibility of total transfers, and no effect on net transfers. However, changing the indexation of b (profile B) reverses the direction of flexibility. With b linked to earnings, $NT/\bar{y}$ is constant (profile B'), but $T/\bar{y}$ rises as $\bar{y}$ rises (profile B), demonstrating the illusion of increased generosity. Nevertheless it can be seen by comparing profiles A' and B' that the

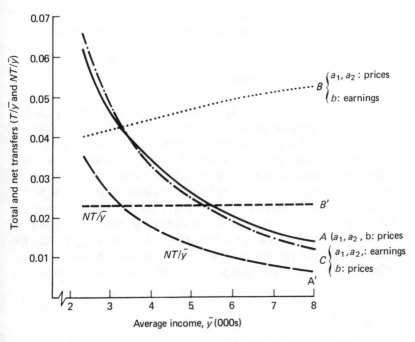

Figure 5.4   Indexation and transfer payments

Source: Creedy and Gemmell (1985)

flexibility of net transfers is sensitive to the form of benefits indexation. The $1\frac{1}{2}$ percentage points decline in $NT/\bar{y}$, mentioned earlier, is removed by increasing the real value of benefits in line with real incomes, instead of holding real benefits constant. However, it is clearly more difficult, by changing the forms of indexation, to ensure that benefits do not become less generous. That is, in the absence of discretionary action by the authorities the built-in flexibility of transfers is more likely to *reduce* their value relative to average income.[6]

Finally, it was suggested in Section 5.2 that changes in the relationship between b, y_B and $\bar{y}$ could be important for policy, and that y_B will rise faster than b if a_1 is indexed by less than b. The simulations confirm that quantitatively these changes can be significant. In the case of profile B in Figure 5.4 indexation of benefits to earnings keeps $b/\bar{y}$ constant as $\bar{y}$ rises. However this causes $y_B/\bar{y}$ to rise from 0.72 at £2500 to 0.76 at £4000 (reaching 0.82 when $\bar{y}$ 8500). Such a rise is significant both because it could be alleged to increase disincentive effects and because it occurs along with a constant 'benefit-earnings' ratio.

5.3.4 Value added tax revenue

In section 5.2 it was suggested that VAT revenues could be expected to decline as $\bar{y}$ rises as a result of an 'income effect' due to income tax changes, and a 'redistribution effect' resulting from different forms of indexation of benefits. In Figure 5.3 it was shown that, without indexation, these combined effects did not reduce VAT revenue at anything like the rate of increase in income tax revenues. Nevertheless, a fall in $R_v/\bar{y}$ from around 10 per cent to 7 per cent occurred over the full range of incomes considered. Simulating the effects of indexing the income tax thresholds (a_1, a_2) and the benefit level (b), suggests that the magnitude of the income effect is slightly less than the redistribution effect of changes in b. In Figures 5.5 the profiles A, B and C indicate the

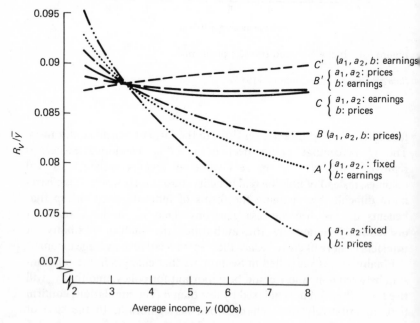

Figure 5.5   Indexation and VAT revenue

Source: Creedy and Gemmell (1985)

effects of changes in income tax indexation, while keeping b indexed to prices. The profiles A', B' and C' show the equivalent profiles with b indexed to earnings.

Consider profile B where both tax thresholds and b are linked to prices. This produces a modest decline in $R_v/\bar{y}$ as $\bar{y}$ rises. It can be seen from profiles B' and C that the increase in the EAR is less as a result of a change in income tax indexation (C), than for a change in benefits indexation (B'). However it is also the case that the increases in EARs of VAT achieved by introducing price indexation (moving from A to B or A' to B') are greater than the further increases achieved by earnings indexation (B to C or B' to C'). This result will, of course, depend on the inflation rate. Notice that *for a given form of income tax indexation*, the increase in the EAR achieved by changing benefits indexation is less, the more income tax is indexed. For example a change in benefits indexation can significantly increase EARs when a_1, a_2 are not indexed (A to A'), but when a_1, a_2 are indexed to earnings, changing the indexation of b has relatively little effect on VAT revenue (C to C').

It can also be seen from Figure 5.5 that, as with transfers, it is extremely difficult to generate an *increase* in $R_v/\bar{y}$ as $\bar{y}$ rises. Unless income taxes and benefits are indexed to earnings, a decline in VAT revenue relative to average income can be expected. Finally, as expected VAT revenue is not sensitive to the form of NI indexation since the sensitivity of NI revenue to indexation is itself slight.

5.3.5 Net revenue

As may be expected, indexation of thresholds can substantially reduce net revenue for a given value of average income, compared with the non-indexed case. This may be seen in Figure 5.6. For example, in the absence of indexation $R/\bar{y}$ rises from 0.24 to 0.35 as average income increases from about £2600 to £4000, whereas indexation of all thresholds to prices causes the $R/\bar{y}$ schedule to become much less steep, rising from 0.30 to 0.32. Relative to the non-indexed case, alternative forms of indexation do not have very different effects on net revenue. In addition, compared with the full earnings indexation of all thresholds (giving a constant $R/\bar{y} = 0.313$), the indexation of any threshold in line with prices cannot substantially increase $R/\bar{y}$. Only non-indexation creates sizeable built-in flexibility. Nevertheless net revenue sensitivity varies among forms of indexation of benefits, as may be seen by the shift from Profile B to C in Figure 5.6. With benefits linked to prices,

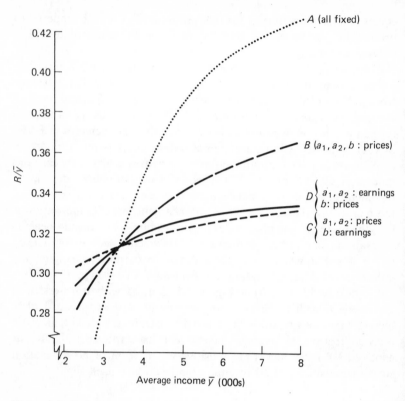

Figure 5.6 Indexation and net revenue

Source: Creedy and Gemmell (1985)

as $\bar{y}$ rises from £2600 to £4000, $R/\bar{y}$ increases from 0.296 to 0.323 (profile B). With earnings indexation of b, $R/\bar{y}$ increases from 0.306 to 0.319 (profile C). A loss of 1 per cent of revenue (relative to average income) could represent a substantial revenue reduction. Thus from the point of view of tax revenue it is important for decisions on indexation of benefits to be taken in conjunction with decisions on income tax indexation.

Finally the results show that declining EARs of National Insurance and VAT (and increasing effective average transfer), are not sufficient to outweigh the increasing EAR of income tax. Hence, except with indexation of all thresholds to earnings, effective average rates of tax must rise, even if only slightly, as average income rises. This occurs because declining EARs of NI and VAT are in any case small, and because maximum upward transfer payments flexibility (which reduces net revenue) occurs with, and partly because of, maximum income tax flexibility (which considerably increases revenue).

5.4 SUMMARY AND CONCLUSIONS

This chapter has examined how revenue from a tax system of direct and indirect taxes can be expected to change in the presence of income growth. A model of interdependent taxes was used including income tax, National Insurance, value added tax and a simplified system of income transfers to the low paid taking the form of a guaranteed minimum income. These components are common features of many tax systems but the model used specific tax forms and parameter values which approximated the UK system. Using a lognormal distribution of incomes in conjunction with the tax functions, results were obtained for tax revenues for a range of average incomes.

It was argued in Section 5.2 that revenue growth for particular taxes in an interdependent system will be affected, not only by the extent of the adjustment of thresholds for the tax concerned, but also by the adjustment of the thresholds of other taxes. It was shown that in the UK tax thresholds and benefit levels have tended to be adjusted by some form of indexation to price or nominal earnings changes. To enable comparisons of revenue growth under different indexation assumptions, three forms of indexation of thresholds and benefit levels were used: fixed (that is, no indexation); adjustment at the rate of growth of prices; and adjustment at the rate of growth of nominal earnings.

The results obtained in Section 5.4 allow some general observations to be made on the effects of economic growth on revenue from the tax/transfer system. It was shown that without any indexation of thresholds substantial increases in income tax revenue (as a proportion of average income), $R_i/\bar{y}$, accompanied increases in average income, for given tax rates. Conversely the total value of transfers fell rapidly as a proportion of average income. National Insurance and VAT revenues, however, displayed relatively little built-in flexibility being only slightly regressive and progressive taxes respectively. The income tax flexibility dominates the flexibility of the tax system as a whole and therefore total tax revenue flexibility was found to be broadly similar to that of income tax.

A common feature of the various tax revenue schedules was that indexation (to either prices or earnings) substantially reduced revenue flexibility. This occurred at what may be regarded as fairly modest rates of price and earnings growth (5 per cent and 7 per cent respectively) by recent historical standards. Most revenue schedules also displayed a tendency for revenue to change rapidly at low values of $\bar{y}$, but schedules 'flattened' considerably at higher $\bar{y}$ values. This would seem to indicate that, given this type of tax structure, revenue flexibility is likely to be much greater at lower per capita income levels than at higher levels. Indeed it seems that, *ceteris paribus*, tax authorities will have to rely increasingly on discretionary instruments rather than automatic changes to increase tax revenues as incomes grow.

Thirdly, it appears to be difficult to generate increases in VAT revenue as incomes grow. While VAT revenue is sensitive to different forms of indexation of income tax and transfers, the unlikely combination of earnings indexation of income tax thresholds and transfer payments is required, to produce a rising VAT revenue schedule. A similar phenomenon occurs with transfer payments. If the benefit level, b, is indexed to earnings, total transfers paid can rise as a proportion of average income. However this only occurs if income tax thresholds are indexed at less than the rate of growth of earnings, and *net* transfers as a proportion of average income will, at best, remain constant. Further it was found that indexation at less than earnings growth, especially of the benefit level, produces sizeable falls in $T/\bar{y}$ and $NT/\bar{y}$. Therefore if 'poverty' relief is to be maintained, while the real burden of taxation rises, (because of, for example, the built-in flexibility of income tax) discretionary action is required to adjust benefit levels or other social security variables.

Finally total (net) revenue was found to rise relative to average income as incomes grew even if *some* tax/transfer thresholds were indexed to earnings. Obviously if all thresholds were indexed to earnings there is zero flexibility but it was found that earnings indexation of either income tax thresholds *or* transfers can still be expected to significantly increase net revenue as incomes rise, and especially at lower average income levels. For the same reason net revenue is most sensitive to income tax and transfers indexation, but fairly insensitive to indexation of VAT and National Insurance.

These results, while derived from a model of a specific tax system, are useful for analyses of other tax systems. The income tax schedule for example was shown in Chapter 4 to be very flexible and hence readily applied to alternative income tax structures. Social insurance taxes similar to the National Insurance system are used in many countries. The model can incorporate if necessary a progressive social insurance tax (making it more like income tax) and can accommodate the additional interdependence where the tax base for the social insurance tax is post-income-tax income. Thus this method of modelling tax revenue growth can be applied to various tax systems in use. It can identify in particular the consequences of different interdependencies between taxes and indexation policies, for the flexibility of tax revenues. This is clearly of importance for countries experiencing structural changes involving a growth of the public sector which are financed from public revenues.

Part III
Service Sector Growth in Egypt and Other Less Developed Countries

Part 3 of this book concentrates on the growth of services in *less developed* countries, and the emphasis is on case studies of individual countries to complement the cross-section evidence discussed in Part 2. This helps to identify some of the influences on service sector growth in less developed countries and highlights both the similarity and diversity of their experience of this increasingly widespread phenomenon.

As shown in Chapter 2, several LDCs have experienced structural changes which have been heavily towards service activities. Most are in Latin America and Asia and have received more attention in previous research. Case studies on the service sectors in a number of these countries are reviewed in Chapter 6, and this is followed in Chapters 7 and 8 by a more detailed examination of the extent of, and influences on, the recent growth of service industries in Egypt. Some consequences of the growth in Egypt's non-marketed services in particular, are also considered in Chapter 9, using the framework described in Chapter 3.

6 Evidence from African, Asian and Latin American Studies

6.1 INTRODUCTION

Evidence from Chapter 2, and studies referred to there, clearly indicate a substantial growth in service activities, in many developed and developing countries. This recent rise in the contribution of services to economic activity in both groups of countries has led to a number of detailed studies aimed at identifying the characteristics, causes and consequences of service sector growth. It is only since the 1970s, however, that the phenomenon has been recognised as fairly widespread in *developing* countries, whereas in developed countries (especially the USA) service sector growth has been studied since the early post-World War II period. The work of Fabricant (1952), Stigler (1956) and Fuchs (1965, 1968) represented early attempts to develop the 'economics of tertiary industry' as Clark (1940) put it, but were based almost exclusively on the USA.

During the 1970s as service growth in more countries began to be documented in greater detail, studies of developed and developing countries tended to follow different approaches. Indeed the phenomenon of service growth itself seems to be rather different in each group of countries. In developed countries service expansion has generally been associated with increased 'modern' services such as banking and insurance and the expansion of the public sector. In addition *relative* service sector growth has frequently occurred with an *absolute* decline in employment in (and sometimes output from) the manufacturing sector. In studies of developing countries, on the other hand, it is 'informal' services which have received most attention. These services are almost always privately produced, could not be termed 'modern' by usual definitions of the term, and have grown simultaneously with an absolute increase in manufacturing activities. In fact it is the informal sector as a whole (including goods production) rather than services *per se* which has been the focus of much research. Within empirical studies of the informal sector 'small-scale manufacturing' has frequently been the main activity investigated despite the increasing evidence (discussed below) that service activities dominate the informal sector.

This chapter brings together evidence from a number of studies of the service sectors in *developing* countries. This allows a general assessment of the evidence (in Chapter 10) and comparisons with evidence from Egypt, which is studied in detail in Chapters 7 to 9 below.

An examination of previous case studies of service sector growth reveals that the methodologies adopted are very different. Firstly, studies can be classified according to whether they (a) set out to examine service sectors (in general or particular sub-sectors), or (b) set out to examine the informal sector, and *de facto* provide evidence on informal service activities. This division is reflected in the organisation of this chapter: Section 6.2 considers 'service sector' studies of India, Israel, Philippines and Taiwan, Singapore, and Colombia, while Section 6.3 presents evidence on service activities within the informal sector. These include studies of Africa (Kenya, Nigeria, Sierra Leone, Togo), Asia (India, Indonesia, Philippines, Sri Lanka) and Latin America (Argentina, Brazil, Colombia).

Secondly methodologies differ with respect to the sector or sectors with which service activities are compared. Thus for example Berry's (1978) study compares service growth in Colombia (and other Latin American countries) in the 1960s with that in developed countries at a similar stage in their development. Alternatively Seow (1979) compares services with manufacturing in Singapore, while Ofer (1967) and Sinha (1968), (Israel and India respectively) examine why the size/growth of the service sector differs from contemporary international patterns.

Finally some studies seek only to document the evidence on the size or growth of service activities while others also attempt (with varying degrees of success) to identify causes. These differences in approach make inter-country comparisons of evidence, or identification of common causes, difficult. Nevertheless, some interesting parallels of experience are evident across countries and these are explored in Chapter 10. First, however, we turn to evidence from some service sector case studies.

6.2 SERVICE SECTOR STUDIES

This section summarises the evidence and conclusions from five studies of service sector growth in six less developed countries. These are Sinha's (1968) examination of trade and commercial services in India; a study by Ofer (1967) of services in general in Israel; Bhalla's (1970) comparison of 'modern' and 'traditional' services in the Philippines and Taiwan; an evaluation of service sector growth in Singapore by Seow; and finally a study of service expansion during urbanisation in Colombia, by Berry (1978). In each case the study has been prompted by the unexpected or unusual nature of the sector's development. It should be noted, however, that it has not always been particularly rapid growth in services which has attracted attention. In the case of the Indian and Singapore studies unexpectedly slow growth was observed.

6.2.1 India

Sinha's interest was in *trade and commerce* services, which in 1961 accounted for over one-fifth of the male non-agricultural labour force in India. From census data Sinha noted that during 1951–61 although the male labour force in trade services rose by around 10 per cent, this represented a fall in the sector's share of (male) employment, from around 6 per cent to 5 per cent. Given the substantial increases in agricultural production and industrial output over the period, together with the increased monetisation of the economy, this relative decline was surprising. A sizeable increase in the flow of commodities through the trade sector could have been expected during the period, and yet, in employment terms, the sector experienced a relative contraction. This followed a stable share in employment from 1901–1931, and a large rise in employment between 1931 and 1951 which increased the sector's employment share.

Sinha's study is one of few, which utilises cross-section as well as time-series data, by examining employment change across Indian states. He found that the relative employment decline observed for India as a whole was experienced by all states except Assam. The relative employment decline therefore seems to be spatially fairly general. However, separating trade and commerce services into three categories – trade in foodstuffs; trade in other commodities; and miscellaneous trade and commerce (insurance, foreign trade, real estate), the employment decline was found to be concentrated in other commodities trade. Employment rose by over 40 per cent and 20 per cent in food and miscellaneous trade respectively but fell absolutely by about 12 per cent in non-food trade, 1951–61. Thus it appears that only non-food trade employment failed to respond in the expected manner to the development of the Indian economy.

Sinha considers four potential influences on the commodities trade sector: (a) productivity in the goods sector, (b) urbanisation, (c) organisational changes in trade, and (d) alternative job opportunities. The first two categories are incapable of explaining the employment decline since evidence of increased goods productivity and urbanisation over the period should serve to increase rather than decrease trade service employment. Sinha argues, however, that there is some evidence of organisational changes within trade. This took the form of 'pedlars and hawkers' being replaced by regular shops, with a concomitant shift from family to commercial production. This shift could be expected to be associated with a rise in the share of wage employment in trade. Examining inter-state data Sinha finds that, indeed, for urban areas, the decline in the relative employment in trade is significantly and negatively correlated with the share of wage employment in total trade employment.

Finally it is argued by Sinha that much of the surplus labour from agriculture which moved into trade occupations during 1931–51, was able to move out of trade, 1951–61, because of increased alternative job opportunities. There does appear to be some association between the rate of growth of wage employment *outside* trade and the relative decline in trade employment. In addition relatively low wage rates in retail trade may have encouraged some movement of wage labour out of this sector.

It would seem then that productivity improvements in parts of the trade sector in excess of those achieved in the goods sector were primarily responsible for the observed relative decline in trade employment. These productivity gains were achieved mainly by organisational changes resulting from the development of the Indian economy over the period and the associated economies of scale. This enabled trade sector output to rise, with relatively slow employment growth in the (non-food) commodity trade sub-sector. A note of caution should, however, be raised regarding the data. By considering only the *male* labour force, Sinha's data may be biased. In particular it is possible that a relative decline in male trade employment may simply reflect relatively greater female participation in trade over the period. Informal sector studies elsewhere have confirmed that female participation is often greater in the informal sector compared to the modern sector, and that within the informal sector, females can be concentrated in trade services. (See, for example, Jurado *et al.*, 1981.)

6.2.2 Israel

The methodology adopted by Ofer (1967) in his study of services in Israel was to compare the shares of services in output and employment with those predicted for a country at Israel's stage of development, from international evidence. Using regression analysis on cross-country data similar to Kuznets (1957) and Chapter 2 above, Ofer obtains predicted shares for service employment (including various sub-sectors) which are considerably below those pertaining in Israel in 1961. Israel was found to have an employment share in all services of about 50 per cent (compared with a prediction of 36 per cent), of which 30 per cent was in public 'other services' (general government, health, education, etc.) which were predicted at 20 per cent. Ofer seeks to explain these unusually high service sector shares.

The evidence on the excessive shares of services (or 'overconcent-ration' in services as Ofer terms it) may be summarised as follows:

(a) For the country's income level (in 1961) there was an overconcent-ration in services in terms of employment and output. Service productivity, as measured by output per man was in line with predictions. This was true for the main service subsectors (trans-port, commerce, public services, personal services), including those where there was sizeable excess employment.

(b) Overconcentration of employment was mainly within the public services of general government, education, health, welfare and religious services. There was some overconcentration in transport and commerce but particularly in trade services this appeared to be small.

(c) Historical evidence from the period 1931–61 suggested the over-concentration was present since the 1930s. However, at the begin-ning of the period the service 'excess' was primarily in trade and personal services, and no overconcentration was observed in general government services.

(d) Public services expanded particularly after the establishment of the State in 1948, but apart from general government were overcon-centrated as early as 1931.

Ofer suggests that the factors determining this excess service employ-ment are of three sorts – foreign trade effects on industrial structure, factors specific to public services, and the occupational structure of immigrants.

Foreign trade can affect industrial structure in three ways. Firstly, where a country has an 'import surplus' (that is, an excess of imports over exports), total per capita resources exceed per capita incomes. Countries' service shares should therefore be compared using per capita resources rather than per capita national income. Ofer terms this 'the income effect'. Secondly, since imports (and exports) are more goods-intensive than domestic production, an import surplus is likely to induce a shift in domestic production towards services, that is, a 'substitution effect'. Finally, Ofer suggests that countries with a comparative advantage in services may specialise in service production.

Ofer found that the income effect could explain about 4 percentage points (or under 30 per cent) of the 14 percentage points service overconcentration discussed in (a) above. Within services, however, there were sizeable differences, with 80 per cent of the transport and commerce excess 'explained', but only 15 per cent of 'other services' excess 'explained'. In addition the import surplus had generally declined since the 1930s which is consistent with the reduction in overconcentration in trade services identified in (c) above.

Empirically it is difficult to separate the substitution and specialisation effects of foreign trade but it is argued by Ofer that together these effects probably accounted for over half of Israel's excess service employment in 1961. However, although imports contain relatively few (final) services as a whole, they contain considerably more transport and commerce services than 'other services'. The substitution effect is thus concentrated in the latter.

It was noted earlier that the bulk of excess service employment was in publicly-provided 'other services'. Ofer argues that a number of factors specific to the public sector help explain this. Firstly, government expenditure has been able to expand rapidly since the establishment of the state because of 'considerable non-tax revenues'. Only about one half of government expenditure is financed by taxation, a quarter coming from domestic non-profit organisations (set up in the pre-State period), and a further quarter from 'foreign sources'. Israel is unlike most other LDCs in this respect since Israel's foreign income to the public sector can not be equated with the international borrowing which has become a feature of other LDCs deficit financing in recent years.

A number of *factors specific to the public sector* are identified by Ofer. For education services, where much of the public sector 'excess' exists, it is argued that 'Israel combines the demographic characteristics of an underdeveloped country with the educational standards of a developed one'. Israel's population growth rates are fairly typical of LDCs, giving a population of school age to total population ratio of around 32 per cent in the early 1960s. However, perhaps because of the developed country origins of many Jewish immigrants, there have been strong demands for a well-developed education system. In 1961 the number of pupils per teacher in Israel was among the lowest in the world. Thus total education expenditures (and employment) are necessarily high.

A similar 'problem' seems to exist in health services – health provision standards are high while the health of immigrants is often poor. According to Ofer this is largely because of government objectives of high health standards (made possible by the non-tax funds available) and the 'free' provision of many services, which boosts demand. In addition the Israeli health system makes intensive use of doctors, but small use of hospitals, so encouraging a labour-intensive provision. This is mainly due to the high immigration rates of qualified doctors and welfare workers.

The growth in 'general government' services is attributed by Ofer to (a) pressure to absorb the unemployed (often resulting from high immigration) into the public sector; (b) ideological favouring of public sector expansion by the social democratic government then in power; and (c) inability to reap significant economies of scale in public service provision due to Israel's small size. For this to explain higher *relative* employment in government it is, of course, necessary to show that greater economies of scale are available in other sectors.

Some of the effects of the *occupational structure of immigrants* have been mentioned above. Over the 1931–61 period over 70 per cent of the increase in the Jewish population came via immigration. The occupational structure of immigrants was generally quite different from that of the indigenous population with an especially high proportion of immigrants in trade and the 'liberal professions'. Although many immigrants did change occupations on arriving in Israel, Ofer suggests that the high opportunity cost of retraining led many to seek employment in their existing occupations, accepting low wages in occupations where they created excess labour supply. In addition, as noted above the government in this period was clearly willing to absorb much of this excess supply of doctors, teachers, etc.

In summary, Ofer's evidence suggests that much of Israel's service expansion was due to the effects of trade and immigration. This latter factor is not shared by most other LDCs, but it is interesting to note that some of the problems which it caused (such as the public sector absorption of the otherwise unemployed) are similar to those resulting from rural to urban migration in other LDCs.

6.2.3 Philippines and Taiwan

The studies of India and Israel considered so far highlight the coexistence of 'modern' services (such as formal education and health services, department stores, etc.) and 'traditional' services (such as petty trading, small-scale goods transportation, domestic services, etc.) in LDCs. One aim of Bhalla's (1970) study was to examine the development of these two types of service activities, and the factors influencing their growth.[1] An interesting feature of the choice of Philippines and Taiwan for Bhalla's study is that service employment expanded considerably in both countries but in association with low and high rates of economic growth in Philippines and Taiwan respectively. During the period of study, 1955–65 (Philippines: 1958–64) services accounted for 34 per cent of additional employment in Philippines and 46 per cent in Taiwan. In Philippines the most rapidly growing services were government, community business and recreation services and commerce. Similarly, in Taiwan rapid growth occurred in government services and 'the professions'.

Data limitations forced Bhalla to approximate employment in the modern and traditional components of services (and other sectors) by wage-earning employment and self-employment-family workers respectively. Bhalla found that in Philippines although the ratio of self-employment to wage-employment was falling (1958–64) in agriculture, manufacturing and commerce, there were large rises in the ratio in personal services and construction. These two sectors had particularly slow rates of wage-employment growth; in domestic service wage-employment actually declined. In Taiwan all sectors experienced a decline in the ratio of self-employment to wage-employment. In commerce, and especially retail trade, where traditional services had been prominent, the decline in the ratio was associated with very large rates of increase in wage-employment compared to other sectors. Bhalla, therefore, suggested that 'the relative growth of self-supporting labour varies inversely with the growth of wage-earning opportunities'. Thus in Philippines the generally slower growth meant slow rates of growth of modern sector jobs which encouraged traditional services to expand. In Taiwan, on the other hand, rapid growth in 'modern' jobs caused the composition of services to change away from traditional services.[2] The shift between modern and traditional activities does not, however, seem confined to services.

Bhalla's conclusions from these two opposing trends are best summarised in his own words:

These two phenomena suggest (a) that the inter-sectoral flows of labour in the less developed countries need not always imply labour transfers from agriculture to industry or to services bypassing industry, and (b) that, in fact, labour transfers occur in two stages. In an economy such as the Philippines where the rate of growth of industrial output is relatively slow, the surplus agricultural labour shifts to traditional manufacturing and from there to traditional services when manufacturing expands under conditions of modern technology. At higher rates of growth, however, as in the case of Taiwan, the potential surplus labour of traditional services is absorbed in industry at the same time as the growth of industry generates 'modern' employment in complementary services. The net effect of these movements in opposite directions would be to raise the share of modern employment without necessarily raising the amount of total labour absorption in services. The rate of transformation of traditional into modern types of labour will depend on the rate at which the two contrary processes take place as a result of industrial growth (Bhalla, 1970, pp. 538–9).

Finally, Bhalla investigated differences in sectoral productivity trends between the two countries. He found that in general the average rate of productivity increase was low in Philippines compared to Taiwan. However, in Taiwan there was evidence of a relative productivity gain in goods sectors (including transport and communications) compared to services, whereas in Philippines all service sectors except commerce experienced relative productivity growth. Bhalla considers that this slow growth in productivity in commerce may indicate some underemployment, but if so, faster productivity growth in other services in Philippines is difficult to explain.

6.2.4 Singapore

Singapore is an interesting example for a case study of the service sector since in many respects the country is quite different from the 'typical' LDC. It is a city-state with few agricultural workers, the labour force is mainly wage-earners, and government services are unimportant, contributing only 7 per cent of GDP (or 11 per cent of service sector GDP) in 1973. Services as a whole, however, dominate the economic structure contributing about two-thirds of total employment and more than two-thirds of Singapore's total output.

Examining the growth of service and manufacturing employment in Singapore since the 1920s, Seow (1979) considers, after taking account of data difficulties, that the service sector employment share was probably stable around 70 per cent, 1921–57, but declined from the 1960s to about 63 per cent in 1978. A similar pattern was evident in GDP. As noted earlier such a decline is contrary to international experience of service sector growth during economic development. Two factors are suggested by Seow which may account for this relative decline. Firstly, the absolute size of Singapore's service sector,[3] coupled with the encouragement of industrialisation since the early 1960s, would make it difficult for services to increase or even maintain their share. Interestingly, however, Hong Kong, under similar conditions appears to have maintained its service share, though in 1976 services only accounted for 44 per cent of total employment.

Secondly, it is suggested that the withdrawal of the British military presence from Singapore caused a contraction in activities, mainly service in nature, previously generated by that military expenditure. Military spending is alleged to have accounted for some 10 per cent of service employment and 20 per cent of service sector GDP in the mid-1960s.

Inter-sectoral productivity differences (measured by output per man) were also examined by Seow. It was found that these moved strongly in favour of services and away from goods during the 1961–77 period. From a productivity growth rate in goods sectors 3.8 percentage points faster than in services, 1961–66, the situation changed to a services productivity growth rate of 3.1 percentage points faster than in goods, 1973–77. Thus, contrary to usual arguments, factors causing productivity growth appear to be greater in services. Using growth-accounting techniques Seow found that only a small proportion of these productivity differentials could be 'explained' by different trends in hours worked in each sector while differences in capital inputs across sectors could explain about a quarter of the observed productivity differences. In fact, differences in all factor inputs across sectors only accounted for around 40 per cent of the productivity differentials, leaving some 60 per cent to be explained by the 'residual' – 'intra-sectoral shifts, internal and external economies of scale and technological change'.

Significant intra-sectoral shifts seem to have been occurring in the service sector since the early 1960s. Seow identifies that commercial, and community/social services were declining in importance, while transport and finance services experienced relative gains. Indeed Seow argues that intermediate services (that is, not sold to final consumers) in general, such as transport, storage, finance, insurance and business services, significantly increased their share of employment and output in the period 1960–78. The share of total service output accounted for by these services rose from 33 per cent in 1960 to almost 50 per cent in 1978. 'Final' services such as retail trade, restaurants/hotels, and social services experienced a similar relative decline. Most of these intermediate services are tradeable and, unlike in most LDCs, make an important contribution to Singapore's balance of payments. Indeed Singapore was able to remain in surplus on the balance of payments, despite a declining trade balance, because of invisible earnings. It seems quite possible that these intermediate/export-orientated services are more technology-intensive than many of Singapore's final services which have been in relative decline, and this may partly account for the service sector's rapid productivity growth.

It does seem that services in Singapore are predominantly in the 'modern' category. Seow suggests that there are more 'white collar' jobs in services than manufacturing, giving higher average wages in the former. Additionally, and contrary to expectations, he found that services as a whole were not more labour-intensive, but seemed to be more capital-intensive, than manufacturing. This is probably partly explained by the concentration of industries in Singapore where the dominant technology is relatively labour-intensive and, according to Seow, the abundance of low-wage 'guest workers' (from surrounding countries) which discouraged capital-labour substitution. Conversely Singapore's service sector does appear to be increasingly concentrated in modern, relatively capital-intensive services. However, there is also evidence of high levels of part-time employment in retail trade and personal services which is suggestive of some 'traditional' services continuing to flourish in Singapore.

In summary, Singapore's service sector is extremely large by international standards but from the 1960s has declined relative to goods sectors in terms of both output and employment. However, it does seem that this was particularly rapid in the early 1960s when the industrialisation drive was strongest. Since the early 1960s productivity and output growth in services has been growing relative to goods which, if it continues, must soon reverse the relative service decline. Within services, intermediate and export-oriented services are much more important than in most LDCs, and increased their share of service output over the period. Undoubtedly the shift towards intermediate services was encouraged by Singapore's industrialisation.

6.2.5 Colombia

The study by Berry (1978) concentrates on Colombia but also draws evidence from other Latin American countries. Berry's concern was primarily to investigate whether the emergence of a service sector in a number of Latin American countries, before widespread industrialisation, was evidence of excessive rural to urban migration. He argues that 'there is at present no reason to believe it [the shift from agriculture to services rather than industry] to be a less efficient process than the historical pattern in now developed countries, where production of goods provided relatively more urban employment than it does today'. To assess the reasons for the high share of services, Berry's methodology is to compare the size and characteristics of the service sector in todays LDCs with those in now developed countries at a similar stage in their development.

Berry found that urbanisation in Latin America was associated with large and often increasing employment in urban service sectors. The shares of the non-agricultural labour force in services in Latin American and other LDCs was also confirmed to be systematically above those pertaining in the USA and European countries at appropriate periods in the nineteenth and early twentieth centuries. Further, Berry could find no evidence that the share of employment in services affects an economy's rate of growth. Comparable service shares to those in Latin American countries were found in such fast growing countries as Japan, Korea and Taiwan.

It is argued by Berry that the high share of service employment in Latin American cities can not generally be attributed to excess migration leading to a large surplus of urban workers who expand the service sector. Colombian (and other Latin American) evidence suggests relatively low unemployment rates for migrants and that migrants are generally 'white collar' workers while urban natives are 'blue collar'. Hence migration is unlikely to lead to considerable competition with urban workers. In any case in Colombia it seems that 'since migrants react rather sensitively to income differentials and employment opportunities, they are unlikely to flood the urban market without regard to the levels of unemployment' (Berry 1978, p. 216).

What then accounts for the historically large urban service employment in Latin America? Berry suggests four possible explanations.

(1) *Greater technical change* over time in agriculture and manufacturing than in services. This is the familiar argument that difficulties in applying (especially capital-intensive) new technologies in services keeps their productivity growth below that of goods sectors and hence,

ceteris paribus, increases relative labour absorption. Thus LDCs can adopt developed country technologies in manufacturing and to some extent in agriculture, which raises those sectors' productivity, but cannot raise productivity similarly in services. In Colombia relative productivity in services, 1938–64, appeared to be declining over time and low when compared to the historical experience of now developed countries (though output shares were comparable). While this could be due to the expansion of employment in services from surplus urban labour, Berry argues this is unlikely because the service relative productivity decline over time is a world-wide phenomenon, and because Colombian data suggest earnings in services are not low compared with manufacturing. Rather Berry finds slow technical progress a more likely explanation of higher service employment.

(2) *Greater occupational specialisation.* Modern technology in developed countries, which LDCs can now adopt, encourages increased occupational specialisation than the technologies of the previous century. This specialisation means that service activities are increasingly separate occupations and no longer secondary or part-time occupations of workers whose main occupation was classified as industrial. The effect is to raise apparent service employment, though total man-hours in services may not have changed. If LDCs do use such technologies this could help to explain the higher share of services observed in developing countries.

(3) *Trade effects.* Berry argues that 'today's LDCs probably trade more, both externally and internally, than their predecessors 100–200 years ago' (p.220), though no evidence is offered for this. Two effects are stressed. Firstly, since LDCs tend to suffer from a comparative disadvantage in manufactured goods, from which the developed countries did not suffer in the last century, they will tend to import a larger fraction of their manufactured goods and hence domestic industrial structure is biased towards services. This argument is similar to that advanced by Ofer in the case of Israel. Secondly, Berry suggests that new technology has been widely used in transport and communications sectors in LDCs which encourages trade and commerce activities. It is, however, unclear why the net effect of this technology should be to expand rather than reduce transport and communications sector employment, nor why trade sectors should be thus encouraged more than goods sectors.

(4) *Less equal income distribution in LDCs.* Though there are few comparable data available Berry suggests that income distribution may be less equal in today's LDCs than at comparable periods in the developed countries. If so, this may help to explain the large size of

domestic service employment, which in 1964 represented about one-third of Colombian service employment. Further Berry notes that the share of employment in domestic services rose rapidly during 1928–51 but only slowly 1951–64 – periods in which income distribution seems to have been worsening and slightly improving respectively.

On the composition of the Colombian service sector Berry found the employment shares of trade, commerce and especially government services and domestic service higher than comparable developed country shares. Transport and communication sectors, on the other hand, did not seem unduly large. Those differences provide some limited support for the four explanations hypothesised above. Nevertheless, Berry recognises that *some* expansion of services was due to the growth of supply-determined services which 'perform a safety valve role for persons with few alternatives' (p. 223).

6.3 INFORMAL SECTOR STUDIES

The ILO (1972) report on Kenya is generally regarded as marking a turning point in the understanding of, and research on, the informal sector. Prior to the report, informal sector activities (often labelled 'traditional') were commonly *assumed* to be primarily of a 'service' type, produced inefficiently and despite the lack of an effective demand for them. The ILO report and subsequent research has shown that the informal sector can be efficient, is not purely supply-determined, and many manufacturing activities are found within the sector. Indeed it is with the productive small-scale manufacturing aspects that much recent research has been concerned. However, there are now several case studies exclusively on informal service sectors, including Moser (1977), Bromley (1978) and Majumdar (1980), as well as many which concentrate on informal services. A number of these latter studies are presented in Sethuraman (1981), and much of this section is devoted to summarising the evidence from these investigations. The evidence presented below is divided into African, Asian and Latin American studies, partly for ease of presentation and partly because certain important differences emerge between the continents.

6.3.1 African countries

The main evidence considered in this section is from Kenya (ILO, 1972, who also present some evidence on 'formal' service sectors), and two studies of urban informal sectors in Freetown, Sierra Leone (Fowler, 1981) and Lagos, Nigeria (Fapohunda, 1981).

Since ILO (1972) defined 'formal' sector employment as that enumerated in official statistics, some of the employment in 'formal' services would undoubtedly be classified as informal using alternative definitions. More recent attempts to define the sector have usually used type of economic activities or various enterprise/individual characteristics to distinguish informal activities, which may or may not be officially enumerated.

For service sectors (which accounted for about 40 per cent of 'formal' employment and GDP in Kenya) ILO (1972) found that wholesale and retail trade was experiencing a change in employment composition away from wage-employment and towards self-employment, 1967–70. This was associated with an absolute decline in wage-employment in the sector, (confirming evidence by Bhalla, 1970) and a rapid increase in average wages in the sector. Indeed ILO consider that the employment fall probably results in part from the large wage rise. However, government licensing restrictions and 'Kenyanisation' may also explain the employment fall to the extent that they encouraged a substitution of small-scale, self-employed African traders for larger 'Asian' shops.

In the 'licensed' transport sector employment also declined (1965–70), mainly in rail transport. This appears to be partly due to short-term local factors though it is also suggested that increased competition from road transport, mostly in the 'unlicensed' (illegal) sector can account for the apparent employment fall. Once again therefore employment declines may be due to a shift towards self/informal employment. ILO (1972) also found that employment in the public sector (which is mainly, but not entirely, in services) had grown at around twice the rate of growth of the private (non-agricultural) sector during 1964–70. This was attributed to post-independence development needs and the 'Tripartite Agreements' in 1964 and 1970 which were partly designed to expand employment. Interestingly, however, ILO conclude that 'the growth of government employment does not seem to be disproportionately large' and that government employment expansion was not an unemployment relief measure. On the other hand it is also suggested that 'casual employment' in the public sector increased by over 40 per cent between 1969 and 1971 which seems unlikely to have been necessary for the public sector to perform its functions.

Finally, in the 'other services' category, including social, business, recreational and personal services, an overall increase in self-employment relative to wage-employment was observed. This was especially the case in 'technical and legal services', probably reflecting the rise in the modern professions, and 'personal services', which probably reflects rising traditional services. Rapid increases in wage employment were, however, evident in social and administration services which is consistent with the evidence above for the public sector, to which most of these services belong.

For the informal sector ILO (1972) were unable to categorise activities into service, manufacturing etc. but undoubtedly services are an important part of the estimated 25–30 per cent of the urban labour force which the informal sector takes. The ILO consider the size of the informal sector to be a direct consequence of migration which caused urban labour force increases to exceed the growth of formal sector income opportunities.

Several similarities in the informal sectors of Freetown, Sierra Leone and Lagos, Nigeria, emerge from the studies by Fowler and Fapohunda. Firstly in sample surveys of informal enterprises both studies found a larger proportion in services, especially trade, than manufacturing. In Freetown trade represented 50 per cent of the sample and manufacturing, 20 per cent. In Lagos the balance was more even with percentages of 46 per cent and 40 per cent in services and manufacturing respectively. An interesting study of Lomé, Togo by Nihan *et al.* (1979) found that although services had more employment in total than 'production' industries this was made up of many fewer 'regular employees' but many more apprentices. Employment growth in services also appeared to be twice as fast as in production industries.

Secondly both Fowler and Fapohunda found that most enterprises had no, or very few, employees. The trade sector had particularly few employees. However, enterprises often had unpaid apprentices, around 50 per cent of whom in Lagos left the enterprise after training, usually to set up their own enterprise. Both studies also found that most entrepreneurs were migrants (as much as 95 per cent in Lagos), and that between 23 per cent and 30 per cent of these migrants had arrived in the towns within the previous five years. The number of enterprises appeared to be growing fairly rapidly, with 18 per cent of Fapohunda's sample setting up in the year preceding the survey. Finally Fowler noted, 'the entry point for a large majority of informal sector entrepreneurs is the trade and repair activities and that many of them manage to penetrate into other sectors in time' (p. 67).

Nihan *et al.* (1979) provide some useful evidence on Lomé's 'modern' informal sector – informal activities producing goods and services similar to those of the modern formal sector. As noted above, services are prominent in this informal sector and repair services are particularly important. Nihan *et al.* found that modern informal sector employment (including apprentices) was equivalent to about 50 per cent of formal sector employment. In addition they found that one-third of former informal apprentices later move into the formal sector. Interestingly, for employees in general, movements from formal to informal sectors were not uncommon. Nihan *et al.* also argue that participation in the sector does not represent disguised unemployment, with almost three-quarters of their sample being better off than in equivalent formal sector employment. This is similar to Fowler and Fapohunda's findings that *entrepreneurs* earn incomes well in excess of minimum (official) wage levels, though this is often not the case for *employees*. Finally labour productivity is low in the informal sector compared to formal enterprises, but given lower capital inputs this is to be expected.

6.3.2 Asian countries

This section summarises evidence from Sri Lanka (by the Marga Institute, 1981), Indonesia (by Moir, 1981), Philippines (by Jurado *et al.*, 1981) and India (by Majumdar, 1980). These studies indicate some interesting differences and similarities between African and Asian informal sectors.

One difference concerns the service component of informal sector employment. This seems to be even larger than in most African countries. In Colombo, Sri Lanka, services (including trade) were estimated to form 91 per cent of informal employment, with manufacturing providing only 5 per cent. The services share in Manila, Philippines was estimated at 85 per cent by Jurado *et al.* Majumdar (1980) does not provide an industrial breakdown of informal employment in India but it is clear that services dominate there also though almost certainly less so than in smaller Asian countries.

Another feature of Asian informal sectors is that while most enterprises were begun by migrants, in the majority of cases these were not recent migrants. Colombo has witnessed very little migration in recent years causing slow growth in the informal sector. Marga Institute (1980) argue that this is due in large part to slow growth in urban incomes in general which has discouraged migration, and increasing numbers of educated among the unemployed who find informal employment unattractive. Similarly, in Jakarta, Indonesia, over 60 per cent of migrants in the informal sector had been in the city more than ten years, at the time of the survey. This evidence is consistent with the generally lower birth rates that have been found for informal enterprises in Asian, compared to African, countries.

Certain similarities between African and Asian informal activities are also evident. Trade services also seem to dominate in informal services in Asia. They formed 63 per cent of the Marga Institute sample, being mainly trade in perishable commodities (e.g. fruit, vegetables, fish). Repair services were again found to be important; and most enterprises had few employees, as in the African studies. This was true even of Colombo, where employees formed 82 per cent of the *total* labour force in 1977, but only about 20 per cent of informal employment. The Asian studies also reveal that most of the enterprises sell their output directly to final consumers, that most entrepreneurs/ employees found their present job without much effort (i.e. entry is relatively easy); and that while the returns to entrepreneurs are relatively high, employees' wages are often below the legal minimum, especially in service sectors. Jurado *et al.* found that in the informal trade sector average employees per enterprise was around 3 but on average only one employee was paid – the other two being unpaid family members or apprentices. Most enterprises in this sector were owned by middle-income households.

Majumdar's Indian evidence provides two further points of interest. Firstly recent migration is more important in India for informal sector growth but this is increasingly *urban to urban* migration. Secondly, the growth of several informal services appears to be associated with increasing demand from greater numbers of middle-income urban dwellers. Majumdar argues that increased provision of childcare services, housekeepers, and laundry/ironing services, for example, reflects increased participation of women from middle-income households in the labour force, and the changing urban life-style in general.

6.3.3 Latin American countries

Latin American countries are generally among the more developed of the developing countries in terms of per capita incomes, and this is reflected in the development and characteristics of informal activities.

In some urban centres the informal sector has developed sufficiently to become similar in many respects to formal enterprises. Thus Sanchez *et al.* (1981) in their study of Cordoba, Argentina, found it necessary to distinguish between 'informal' and 'quasi-formal' activities, defined as 'low' and 'high' income sectors respectively within the small-scale sector (that is, less than five employees). Quasi-formal sector participants, including doctors, lawyers, plumbers, electricians, construction workers, etc., were found to be relatively highly skilled, and educated, had generally been resident in urban areas much longer than informal sector workers, and had greater job/income security. Clearly these activities, many of which are services, have much in common with the 'modern' services in developed countries and reflect the 'middle-income' status of certain Latin American countries.

In common with many established urban centres in Latin America immigration into Cordoba seems to be declining. Migrants were, however, found to be strongly represented in the informal sector, which in Cordoba was composed mainly of services (55 per cent) and trade (20 per cent). In addition it seems that migrants are more likely to move from low income to high income (quasi-formal) activities the longer their duration in the urban centre. Nevertheless informal entrepreneurs (there are few employees) appear to earn relatively low incomes, often below minimum legal wages in formal sectors, and operate from their own residential premises rather than business premises. The opposite holds in general for the quasi-formal sector.

Berlinck *et al.* (1981) found similar evidence of a fairly well developed informal sector in Campinas, Brazil. They found informal enterprises with large amounts of capital compared to that usually found in the informal sector. Owners tended to be skilled workers and were able to earn incomes well above legal minimum wages. Most entrepreneurs had, in fact, learned their skills in the formal sector and moved to the informal sector for better incomes. However, since Berlinck *et al.* also found that most enterprises had a fixed location, were legal and paid taxes, these would seem more like the quasi-formal sector enterprises discussed above. As in Cordoba, most informal entrepreneurs in Campinas were migrants but most had been in Campinas more than ten years and had migrated from other urban centres to the city.

It seems, however, that the evidence of a relatively skilled, high-income informal sector in this case is partly because of the type of urban centre chosen. Campinas is a small, relatively well developed city with only 2 per cent of its population estimated to be living in slums.

Evidence from a larger urban centre with greater numbers of poor residents, by Merrick (1976), suggests an informal sector in which incomes and skill levels are much lower. Merrick's study of Belo Horizonte revealed that the informal sector absorbed many migrants but at relatively low incomes – around 60 per cent of comparable formal sector earnings. More migrants had arrived in the city recently and, as in Cordoba, were able to move into formal sector jobs after some years. Also, unlike Campinas where most participants in the informal sector were secondary earners, in Belo Horizonte more participants were heads of their households and therefore the primary earner. This suggests a greater dependence of poor Belo Horizonte households on the informal sector. This evidence would support the conclusion of Berlinck *et al.* that 'the role of the informal sector is highly dependent on the size of the town/city, the role of migration and the stage and rate of economic development of the region' (p. 167).

Finally an interesting feature of informal service employment was found by Bromley (1978) in his study of street traders in Cali, Colombia. Bromley found that many street traders were selling food-stuffs, manufactured goods, newspapers, etc., produced in the formal sector. Traders were self-employed but often rented capital equipment (such as ice-cream carts) from the formal sector producer. Thus Bromley argues that 'many street traders are little more than disenfranchised employees of larger enterprises'. This provides further support for the view that services appear to take a larger share of economic activity at early stages of development because of limited vertical integration within firms.

6.4 SUMMARY AND CONCLUSIONS

This chapter has presented evidence from a series of case studies of service sectors, and services within the informal sector, in developing countries. Studies of service sectors *per se* have concentrated on Asian and Latin American countries while Africa has been relatively neg-lected. The investigation of services in the Egyptian economy in the following two chapters should therefore provide an African dimension to available evidence. Information from all three continents has accumulated in recent years on the informal sector. Some case studies devoted primarily or exclusively to services, were also reviewed in this chapter. An attempt to assess and compare the results of these studies with those obtained from Egypt is made in Chapter 10 and hence in this section a few limited conclusions are drawn.

One inescapable conclusion is that services dominate the non-agricultural labour forces of many LDCs, and frequently account for a larger proportion of the labour force than manufacturing. This phenomenon is not restricted to those LDCs traditionally regarded as 'service economies', such as Singapore and Hong Kong, but affects many 'typical' LDCs such as India, Brazil and Taiwan. It is also clear that in many cases service activities dominate both formal and informal employment. In formal services government employment is often important, while in informal services the trade sector and personal services seem to be especially large and/or growing rapidly. The trade sector is, however, one in which the formal/informal distinction is particularly difficult to make.

The tendency for the informal sector to flourish when the rate of growth of formal wage-employment was low or even negative was noted in a number of studies, including Sinha (1968), Bhalla (1970) and Berry (1978). This suggests that informal service growth is dependent on the availability of opportunities elsewhere, but this does not necessarily mean that the sector is characterised by substantial disguised unemployment.

Bhalla (1970) and ILO (1972) among others observed a tendency for some services to experience reductions in employment in association with rapidly rising wage rates, and vice versa. There was, however, usually no evidence that wage rate changes *caused* the employment change, though this was presumed in a number of cases. Much more careful examination of the operation of the labour market would seem to be necessary before causation can be identified reliably.

An interesting outcome of the results reported in this chapter is that it is not possible to generalise on productivity differences between service and goods production. Some studies, such as Seow (1979) found service productivity growing more rapidly than in goods sectors, while others (e.g. Berry, 1978, Bhalla, 1970) found evidence of slow service productivity growth. It is possible that high service productivity growth is associated mainly with some 'modern' services such as banking and certain professions while informal services mostly experience slow productivity growth. However, since productivity measures are usually *labour* productivity and capital utilisation varies enormously between these sectors it is difficult to interpret the productivity evidence. Finally the informal sector studies indicate that services in this sector have grown in response to demands from middle-income as well as low-income consumers. Thus the demand for some services such as informal wholesale and retail trade arises mainly from low-income migrants (who may also be the main suppliers). On the other hand laundry and ironing services, domestic service and some street-trading services appear to be purchased primarily by middle-income consumers.

7 Structural Change and Employment Growth: Egypt 1960–75

7.1 INTRODUCTION

The structure of, and structural changes in, the Egyptian economy have been of interest to economists for many years. The development of the cotton industry in Egypt has long been recognised as a source of 'unbalanced' growth and has been studied extensively by, for example, Issawi (1961) and Owen (1969). The growth of the industrial sector overall was the subject of a detailed investigation by Mabro and Radwan (1976), while on structural changes generally Mead (1967), Mabro and O'Brien (1970) and Mabro (1974) have examined resource shifts, involving mainly the agricultural and manufacturing sectors, up till the late 1960s. Using census information Mead (1967) was able to study the development of some services to 1960, but since then, despite widespread recognition of service growth, this sector and the reasons for its relative growth in Egypt have not been studied in detail.

In order to study the growth, relative and absolute, of economic sectors it is, of course, necessary to decide on a *measure* of growth. In Chapter 2 it was suggested that for international comparisons, employment often represented a better measure than output because of such problems as data collection and exchange rate variations. In addition there are well known difficulties associated with measuring service sector output, particularly in the non-market sector. In this case study, therefore, employment is the variable used to measure the size and growth of each sector and it is employment structure which it is sought to explain. Of course, as noted in Chapter 6, empirical investigations of employment structure have often identified output or productivity as important explanatory variables and in the following chapters it is necessary to use data on sectoral output and productivity. For the service sector in particular these data must therefore be interpreted with care.

In the following chapters two classifications of service and industrial activities are used. In this chapter, to enable comparisons with earlier results, agricultural, industrial and service sectors are defined as in

111

Chapter 2, where the industrial sector includes only manufacturing and the service sector is defined, using the 1968 ISIC as transport, communications, finance, wholesale and retail trade and community, social and personal services. In Chapter 8, the approach adopted is to compare all 'service-producing' sectors (and two sub-sectors, 'commercial' and 'social' services), with the 'goods-producing' sector. This approach, first used by Fuchs (1965), while obscuring the details of trends in sub-categories, does enable any general and systematic differences between goods and service sectors, which economic theory suggests may exist, to be identified. Although there are some economic activities which could be classified in either category, (depending on the criteria used) in most cases activities fall clearly into one category. In this study the goods sector is defined to include agriculture, manufacturing, mining and quarrying, electricity, public utilities, construction and housing. (The non-agricultural goods sector is also used for comparisons and is denoted, 'goods*'). The service sector includes 'commercial services' (CS) – transport and communication services, financial services, wholesale and retail trade – and 'social services' (SS) including education, health, government administration and personal services. The terms 'commercial services' and 'social services' are used for convenience and are not necessarily meant to indicate homogeneity within groups. However commercial services predominantly include services which are marketed as opposed to the social service sector which predominantly includes non-marketed services provided 'free' by government (e.g. health services and defence). Using the term 'social services' here avoids the possible confusion of identifying some marketed services in a 'non-market sector'.

The chapter is set out as follows. In Section 7.2 evidence on structural changes for 1960–75 is presented and examined. This is compared to international evidence on structural change and to changes since the early years of the twentieth century. Section 7.3 considers factors which economic theory and previous investigations in other countries have suggested are important explanations of sectoral differences in employment growth. Possible explanations specific to Egypt are also considered. Some of the variables suggested in Section 7.3 are tested in Chapter 8.

7.2 EMPLOYMENT EVIDENCE

7.2.1 The international position

In Chapter 2 it was argued that fairly clear patterns of structural change across countries could be found for agricultural, industrial and service sectors. While some countries deviated substantially from those patterns (e.g. Argentina, Brazil) there was nevertheless a degree of uniformity among a sample of developed and less developed countries. Regression results on these patterns were obtained excluding the Egyptian economy so that it is interesting to compare the structure of Egypt's employment with the international patterns.

Table 7.1 shows the division of employment in Egypt between agricultural, industrial, service and social service sectors in 1960 and 1970. These are compared with the sector shares which are predicted from the international regressions, given the share of employment in agriculture in Egypt in each year. Thus a country with an employment share in agriculture of 54 per cent is predicted to have about 13 per cent and 23 per cent of its employment in industry and services respectively. Social services should make up about two-thirds of the 23 per cent in services. In Egypt, however, industry in 1960 took only 10 per cent of employment, but services absorbed almost 29 per cent. Social services are also more than predicted at almost 18 per cent. Ten years later, in 1970, with a lower employment share in agriculture, Egypt's employment shares in other sectors are all predicted to be higher, as expected.

Table 7.1 Sector employment shares, 1960 and 1970

Year		Agriculture	Industry	Services	Social Services
1960	actual	0.540	0.100	0.287	0.178
	predicted*	—	0.128	0.230	0.157
1970	actual	0.489	0.111	0.330	0.191
	predicted*	—	0.142	0.255	0.168

*Predictions are calculated using equations (i), (ii) and (iii) in Table 2.1(A).

Source: Tables 2.1 and 2.2

Actual figures are higher for all sectors also, but again the service sector is much larger than predicted (33 per cent as against 25 per cent predicted) while industry continues well below predictions.

Of course, domestic factors in particular countries will almost always ensure that in an international comparison some countries lie below and some above the predicted pattern. However comparing Egypt's sector shares with the international sample in Chapter 2, Figure 2.5 shows that Egypt's low industrial share is similar to those less developed countries with the greatest (negative) deviation from the predicted relationship. Egypt's service employment share is considerably above those LDCs which deviate most above the predicted pattern. A comparison of service, social service and industrial employment shares is given in Figure 7.1. This reveals the extent to which Egypt's total and social service sector employment shares (number 1 in each diagram) are in excess of other countries' in the sample, given the size of its industrial sector. Egypt's social service sector in 1970 takes a similar share of employment as such industrialised countries as West Germany, Norway and Australia.

This evidence would seem to suggest that the structure of employment in Egypt, though not unique in its bias away from industry and towards services, is especially unusual by international standards. The particularly large size of social service employment by international standards is also associated with rapid growth during the 1960–1970 period. Chapter 3 provided evidence on the *growth* of market and non-market sector employment for an international sample including Egypt. (For the data used here the non-market and social service sectors are, of course, identical.) This confirmed that, relative to the growth of marketed output, Egypt experienced one of the largest expansions in market and non-market employment, 1960–1970.

7.2.2 Historical evidence

Having obtained some idea of the structural balance in the Egyptian economy in an international context, Egypt's structural balance during the period 1960–75 may be examined in comparison with its earlier economic experience. In particular, it is of interest to know if the imbalance identified in 1960 and 1970 is a phenomenon which developed fairly quickly prior to 1960, perhaps as a result of the upheavals following the 1952 Revolution, or if it existed over a longer period of Egyptian economic history.

115

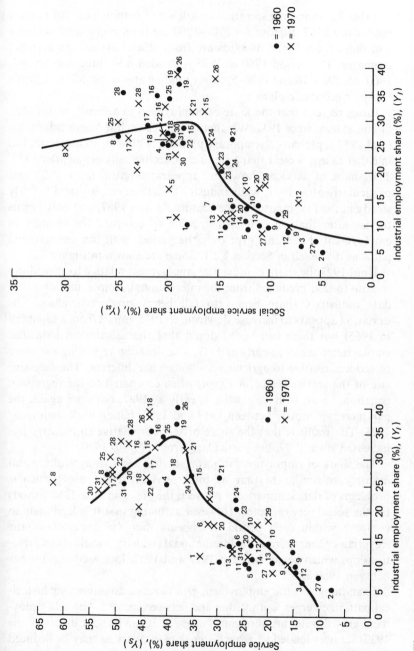

Figure 7.1 Employment in industrial, service and social service sectors, 1960 and 1970

Source: Tables 2.1 and 2.2

Table 7.2 shows the sectoral breakdown of employment for various years since 1907. Figures for 1907–1960 are from population censuses and those from 1960* onwards are from official annual employment estimates. The period 1960 to 1975 is divided into three sub-periods, 1960–65, 1965–70 and 1970–5, corresponding approximately to Egypt's five-year economic plans.[1]

It can be seen that the share of employment in agriculture has been falling at least since 1937. Whether or not the decline began before this (and 1937 represents a temporary upturn), is difficult to ascertain, but in either case it is clear that a significant decline only began after 1937. The share of services, however, appears to grow from 1907 and particularly after 1937, while industry's share of employment is fairly steady in the first quarter of the century, falls in 1937, and only begins to rise after that date. It is interesting to compare the changes in employment shares in Egypt over the period, with the international patterns discussed in Section 7.2.1. Some are shown in Figure 7.2.

Until 1927 the share of industrial employment relative to agriculture is close to that predicted from the international sample, but after that date industry's share begins to fall below predicted values. The deviation appears to increase slowly up to 1975, (apart from a slight fall in 1965) but there can be no doubt that the shortfall in industrial employment began as early as 1947. The situation regarding the share of services relative to agriculture is somewhat different. The excessive size of the service sector in Egypt, when compared to the regression equation, seems to have existed as early as 1907, but once again, the gap increases mostly between 1937 and 1960, falling back slightly by 1975. The result is that the share of services relative to industry has increased since 1907, but particularly from 1937 to 1960.

The share of employment in *social* services *vis à vis* agriculture and industry is similar to that of total services. There are particular problems of data comparisons between the pre- and post-1960 periods for the social service sector. However assuming that it is legitimate to compare within each period, it appears that the deviation of the Egyptian economy from the international industry/social services relationship, which began between 1927 and 1937, increased still further between 1960 and 1975.

Examining sectoral employment *growth rates*, an interesting historical pattern emerges, both within and between sectors. Annual employment growth rates are shown in Table 7.3. It can be seen that until the 1930s services tended to grow faster than industry as may be deduced from the previous share data. From the 1930s, till around 1965, the

Table 7.2 Sectoral shares of employment: Egypt 1907–75

Sector	1907	1917	1927	1937	1947	1960	1960*	1965	1970	1975
Agriculture	68.2	68.0	67.4	69.5	61.6	56.3	54.0	50.9	48.9	44.7
Industry	8.3	8.4	8.2	6.2	8.6	9.4	10.0	11.2	11.1	12.7
Services	20.7	22.0	22.3	22.0	27.8	31.9	32.0	32.3	33.0	35.6
Social Services	13.0	10.9	9.8	12.0	15.8	20.4	17.8	18.6	19.1	20.5

*Figures obtained from labour force sample surveys. Subsequent years are also obtained from this source.

Source: Calculated from data in Mead (1967) and Central Agency for Public Mobilisation and Statistics (CAPMAS), *Statistical Yearbook of the UAR*, Cairo, various issues.

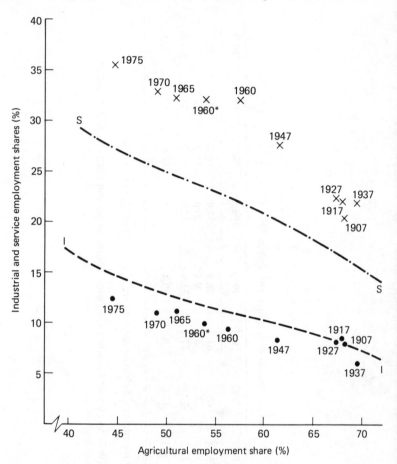

Figure 7.2   Industrial and service sector employment shares: Egypt 1907–75

Source: Tables 2.1 and 7.2

pattern is reversed, however, with industrial growth exceeding service sector growth and a tendency for both sectors to grow faster than previously. After 1965, the pattern changes yet again with industrial growth lagging behind service growth till 1970. The position after 1970 is not clear. Industrial growth over the whole period 1970–75 appears higher than service sector growth (5.1 per cent to 4.2 per cent). However, almost 60 per cent of industrial employment growth in this period, according to official statistics, occurred in the first year 1970–71. For the four remaining years, service growth again exceeded industrial growth with an average annual compound rate of growth for the period of 4.4 per cent in services and 2.8 per cent in industry. Therefore, it would seem that after 1960 industrial employment growth was only growing faster than service employment up to 1965. This was a continuation of a pattern evident since the 1930s, but after 1965 the pattern changes and services (in employment terms) began to grow faster than industry in absolute as well as relative terms.

Table 7.3 also shows the growth of social service employment. Interestingly, for much of the 1927–1960 period, social services appear to grow faster than the industrial sector. After 1960 social services grow at a fairly constant rate (compared to the pre-1960 period) while industrial growth rates fluctuate. Again however after the relatively rapid industrial employment growth 1960–5, (and apart from the 1970–1 year discussed above), social service growth exceeds industrial growth.[2]

Finally, using the analysis developed in Chapter 3 it is possible to put the growth in market and non-market sector employment relative to marketed output in Egypt identified earlier into historical context. It was shown in Chapter 3 that during 1960–70 Egypt's macroeconomic performance in terms of the (weighted) growth rate of non-market employment relative to marketed output, was among the worst in the sample. Figure 7.3 shows these two aspects of Egypt's macroeconomic performance for the period 1947–75. Unfortunately the poor quality of data, and the distorting effect of the Second World War make meaningful comparisons with years before 1947 impossible.

It can be seen in Figure 7.3 that Egypt is on a lower isodifferential line during 1947–60 than that previously identified for 1960–70. However the 1960–70 period displays two very different halves. During 1960–5 Egypt becomes a fairly typical performer but for 1965–70, the substantial reduction in $\dot{Y}_m$ puts the economy on a very low isodifferential line. Between 1970 and 1975 although (weighted) non-market employment growth is higher, simultaneously higher marketed output growth puts the economy in a slightly better position.

Thus it would seem that the poor macroeconomic performance, identified in Egypt for 1960–70 in Chapter 3, existed prior to 1960. Considerable improvements made during the First Five-Year Plan, 1960–5 (in employment terms at least) were not maintained thereafter.

7.3 EXPLANATIONS OF STRUCTURAL CHANGE

Having examined some of the evidence of a relative growth in service sector employment in Section 7.2, in this section possible influences on

Table 7.3 Average annual employment growth rates: Egypt 1907–75

Sector	1907–17	1917–27	1927–37	1937–47	1947–60	1960–5	1965–70	1970–75
Agriculture	2.3	1.9	1.3	0.1	0.8	2.9	1.5	0.8
Industry	2.5	2.1	– 1.7	4.7	2.7	6.5	2.1	5.1*
Services	2.9	2.1	0.8	3.8	2.4	4.4	2.8	4.2
Social Services	0.5	0.8	3.1	4.2	3.3	4.1	4.0	4.7

*Almost 60 per cent of this growth occurred in the first year, 1970–1.

Source: As Table 7.2.

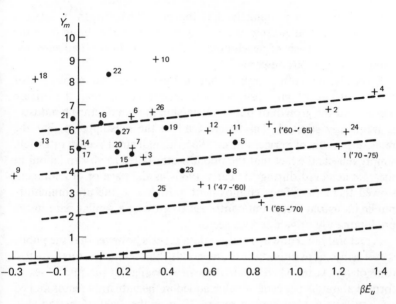

Figure 7.3   Growth in marketed output and non-market employment in 27 countries (1960–70)

Source: Table 3.1

structural change in general are considered. Their relevance in understanding Egypt's structural change may then be investigated. First, however, two factors specific to the Egyptian economy, which may be held to explain the data discussed in section 7.2, are considered.

Firstly, it may be suggested that the relative growth of services after 1965 was simply a return to a longer-term trend, when the drive towards 'industrialisation' during the First Five-Year Plan (1960–5) lost its momentum in subsequent years. While there is some evidence, as will be seen later, that factors causing a growth in services during previous decades did also play a part in the post-1965 growth, they certainly could not be said to explain the whole phenomenon. Both the absolute growth rates of service employment and those relative to industrial employment have fluctuated considerably since the turn of the century. Also, compared to the 1947–60 period, both service sectors grew in absolute terms much faster from 1960 than previously, as indeed did the industrial sector, at least for the first five years. In addition growth in some marketed services relative to the industrial sector occurred for the first time (during the post-war period) only after

1965. Therefore it is unlikely that the post-1965 growth in services could be explained entirely as a resurgence of an earlier trend once the temporary emphasis of development effort on 'industry' had subsided from the mid-1960s onwards.

Secondly, it is often argued that in Egypt when the public sector expands it has a higher propensity to absorb labour than the private sector, and the growth of public ownership in manufacturing industry is frequently stressed. This might lead to the presumption that the relative growth of services after 1965, as industrial sector rates fell, simply reflects the fact that the public sector failed to absorb labour at the rate achieved during the early 1960s as the pace of development slowed thereafter. Thus employment grew less in the predominantly public industrial sector but continued to grow at a similar pace in the predominantly private service sector.

A sectoral breakdown of output data reveals however that the public sector is no more important in the goods than service sectors. In 1974 (one of few years where a breakdown is available) the public sector formed about 68 per cent of value added in the industrial sector and 65 per cent in the total service sector. If, over the 1960–75 period as a whole, public-ownership has extended in industrial sectors more than in services, and it is correct to assume that the public sector is more prone to employ surplus labour, then the observed relative growth of services is *less* than it might otherwise have been. Unfortunately evidence on public ownership changes across sectors is not available. It is clear then that neither of these two explanations is adequate to explain the relative growth in service employment, and an understanding of the relevant causal factors must be sought elsewhere.

The body of literature which has emerged on the expanding share of services in various industrialised western economies has produced several hypotheses. The original arguments of Fisher (1939) and Clark (1940) that income elasticities and productivity differences between sectors are important explanations of the relative growth of service industries as part of the development process continue to have strong support. Other factors which economic theory suggests may cause differential sectoral employment growth include sectoral differences in the elasticities of substitution between labour and capital; and differences in input requirements arising from differential rates of technological progress between sectors or changes in relative factor prices. The effects of different combinations of capital and labour inputs across sectors may of course be evidenced in productivity differences. In the absence of factor substitution, different rates of wages growth between sectors may cause changes in labour allocation. Differences in wages between sectors are, of course, fundamental to many models of structural change, such as Lewis (1954), which sought to explain agriculture to industry shifts.

7.3.1 Income elasticity of demand

The link between income elasticities and differential employment growth between sectors is well documented in the economic literature.[3] It need only be reiterated here that it has been observed that as incomes rise so does the demand for (or consumption of) goods and services. Empirical evidence also suggests that once a certain level of goods consumption has been reached, further increments in income may be used increasingly for greater consumption of services so that there is a tendency for the elasticities of demand for services to rise relative to goods as incomes rise.

Normally, therefore, higher, or a significant increase in, income elasticities for services may be expected to occur only in countries where per capita income is already relatively high and where a high level of goods consumption has been attained, while in Egypt by 1975 per capita national income was only a little over £100 (or approximately $250 at the exchange rates then prevailing). Thus it might be expected that income elasticities will be of little importance in any explanation of faster service employment growth in Egypt. However, two points can be made here. Firstly, in countries where per capita income is not high but where income distribution is very inequitable, it is possible for a minority with high incomes to exhibit high elasticities for services while a majority of those on low incomes are allowed to form only a small part of total market demand. Many writers have pointed to the heavily skewed distribution of income in Egypt, among them Abdel-Fadil (1975) and Radwan (1977) who suggest that land ownership and rural incomes remain very inequitably distributed despite the aims and efforts of the socialist regime. Secondly, it is, of course, possible that the Egyptian consumer exhibits a pattern of income elasticities legitimately inconsistent with that which has been observed in some other LDCs, and it is possible that a 'premature' demand for modern services may arise as some LDCs such as Egypt attempt to emulate 'western' lifestyles. It may be therefore that the relative growth in service sector employment in Egypt since the mid-1960s has been due to a rise in the income elasticity of demand for those services, relative to goods.

7.3.2 Productivity

It has long been argued that productivity growth can be expected to be slower in some services relative to goods-producing sectors with the result that, for equal rates of output growth across sectors, services require faster employment growth. Productivity growth is then argued to be closely linked to technological improvements which may be either exogenous or endogenous. Where technical progress is thought to be exogenous it is suggested that it is more able to affect industrial processes than the production techniques associated with services. On the other hand it is argued that technology embodied in capital has more effect on goods production because it is easier to ally more capital with labour in goods than in service production. Services, it is argued, often depend on 'personal' qualities and therefore need to be more labour intensive. Several criticisms have been made of these arguments not least that the causality between labour intensity and productivity improvements is far from clear; that productivity measures in many services are inadequate; and that in many services considerable productivity gains *can* be made by increased use of capital.

Interestingly some of the arguments for slower service productivity growth may now be more persuasive in less developed than in developed countries. In many LDCs where governments have been involved in planning and/or ownership of production, the objective of 'industrialisation' has led many governments to encourage industrial establishments to grow while ignoring or inhibiting service expansion. Since industrial commodities are often easier to export than services, goods production is encouraged to help balance of payments problems. There may be various consequences for sectoral productivity growth rates from these policies. Firstly, governments may channel investment funds particularly towards manufacturing and related industries enabling faster productivity growth in these sectors, while services are relatively starved of capital. Secondly, governments may encourage larger scale industrial production by various policies while the small-scale service sector is allowed to remain. Thus greater application of capital is possible in industry, and resulting scale economies are obtained. Therefore in some LDCs, government policies rather than technical factors may enable greater capitalisation and productivity growth in industry.

On causality, it is usually argued that, for a given growth in real output, employment growth will be determined by the growth of, exogenously determined, productivity. These three variables are not however independent of each other and there are likely to be causal relationships among them. Higher rates of output growth may, for example, induce higher rates of productivity growth through economies of scale. In Egypt, rather than employment responding to changes in output and productivity as is usually assumed in a mainly private enterprise economy, productivity falls may *result from* excessive employment growth in the public sector in an attempt to relieve unemployment. This effect, which has certainly occurred at some times in Egypt (see Chapter 8) is, however, probably not widespread across industrial and service sectors, where private ownership remains substantial. Where it does occur, it is legitimate to ask why it should be that higher employment growth does not result instead in faster output growth. Numerous factors could be responsible including a lack of demand, or a failure to increase non-labour inputs simultaneously.

7.3.3 Relative factor prices

The role of prices in the determination of quantities is a fundamental principle in economics, particularly in the neoclassical tradition. In the labour market firms may be expected to demand less labour as its price (wages) rise. Where factor substitution is relatively easy, a rise in the price of labour relative to capital will induce a shift in the combination of factor inputs towards capital and away from labour. Where factor substitution is difficult a rise in the price of labour may still result in lower demand for labour, particularly if firms seek to minimise costs or it is difficult to raise sales revenue in line with input price rises.

These effects may be relevant to structural changes in employment. Different rates of growth in wages across sectors (due, for example, to differences in bargaining strength, or skill requirements) may lead to different rates of employment growth, as sectors experiencing more rapid wage increases economise more on their use of labour. Notice that if lower wage rises lead to lower output price increases in these sectors, this may increase demand for those sectors' outputs depending on *price* elasticities of demand. In addition, sectoral output comparisons will differ between real and nominal output measures.

In Egypt the allocative role of factor prices is likely to be complicated by a number of factors. Since the 1950s wage rates have been fixed officially in some sectors but not in others, so that wages may perform different allocative roles across sectors. In some sectors where wages are officially fixed it appears that earnings and even actual rates paid may differ substantially from these. In addition to fixing wage rates some public sector establishments have been given simultaneous employment targets by governments, especially in the early 1960s so that in these instances wages are unlikely to be an important determinant of employment. These and other wage and price controls have existed in Egypt in recent years often covering only some sectors of the economy for limited time periods. It must, therefore, be determined *empirically* whether wage differences are an important determinant of structural change in Egypt.

7.3.4 Relative output prices

Changes in relative output prices can, of course, also produce changes in the structure of employment. A fall in the price of services relative to goods, for example, may induce a shift in consumer demand away from goods and towards services. Any resulting change in output may be expected, via the derived demand for labour, to encourage increased service employment. This effect is enhanced if the elasticity of employment with respect to output is also higher for services than goods, as is often suggested.

Some recent evidence from a sample of countries at various income levels (Kravis, Heston and Summers, 1982) suggests a tendency for the price of services relative to goods to rise as income levels rise. A number of time-series studies for developed countries have also found such a trend for government services.[4] *Ceteris paribus* this would give a high level of real output in services relative to goods at low income levels, which decreases as incomes rise. At least two reasons have been put forward for this phenomenon.

The Kravis-Heston-Summers explanation treats goods and services as, mainly 'traded' and 'non-traded' respectively. Their argument then rests on two assumptions: (i) that traded goods' prices are the same across countries such that wage levels in that sector in different countries will vary according to inter-country differences in productivity; and (ii) that traded goods sector wages determine non-traded sector wage levels. Thus they argue, 'Because international productivity differences are smaller for such (non-traded) industries, the low wages established in poor countries in the low productivity traded goods industries will apply also to the not-so-low productivity service and other non-traded goods industries. The consequences will be low prices in low-income countries for services and other non-traded goods' (p. 21). It is, in fact, far from certain that international productivity differences are less in services than in traded goods as Kravis-Heston-Summers argue, especially if agriculture is excluded. Even if this is the case, the relationship need not hold over time, and it is with the time-series relationship that the present case study is concerned. A second explanation, offered by Bhagwati (1984) for cheaper services in low-income countries, assumes that services technology is more labour-intensive than goods technology in all countries, and that the wage/rental ratio is lower in low-income countries compared to high-income countries. It can then readily be shown that real output of services will be higher relative to goods in low-income countries and that, given internationally determined traded goods prices, services will be cheaper relative to goods in low-income countries.

If services *are* relatively cheaper in low-income countries, and *if* this cross-section evidence is an accurate guide to time-series changes, then, *ceteris paribus* a decline in service real output relative to goods may be expected as incomes rise. This is, of course, contrary to the trends in Egyptian employment identified earlier.

7.4 SUMMARY AND CONCLUSIONS

This chapter has presented some evidence on changes in service employment in Egypt, especially over the period 1960 to 1975. It was shown that apart from the period of the First Five-Year Plan (1960–65) service employment in aggregate grew faster than industrial employment. This was also true of the social service sub-sector. Despite the large size and high growth rates of the service sector relative to industry during the 1960–75 period, historically this does not appear to be unusual. During 1947–60 in particular some services had also grown rapidly, both absolutely and relative to industry.

In an international context the large size of the Egyptian service sector is also apparent. Along with a small number of other LDCs, Egypt's service employment share was found to be atypically large. Indeed it appears to have a service share comparable to a number of developed countries.

For social or non-marketed services it was discovered that the relationship between employment growth rates and marketed output growth rates changed significantly over the 1947–75 period. The macroeconomic performance associated with this relationship was also found to be variable within the period, with 1947–60 and 1965–70 identified as periods of especially 'poor' performance.

Finally Section 7.3 reviewed a number of frequently cited explanations of service sector growth in general, and briefly considered some specific to Egypt. Data problems limit the extent to which some of these general explanations can be pursued in the Egyptian case, but the roles of income elasticity and productivity differences, relative factor prices and relative output prices are examined in Chapter 8.

8 Influences on Service Employment Growth in Egypt

8.1 INTRODUCTION

Evidence on service and industrial employment was presented in Chapter 7. Factors causing differences in employment growth between sectors which economic theory or previous empirical investigation have suggested, were also considered. In this chapter the roles of various explanatory factors in Egypt's employment growth are examined. Rigorous testing of hypotheses on sectoral differences in employment requires a reliable *a priori* economic model, with well specified variables and relationships among them, and a reliable data set. In the case of structural changes in employment although economic theory has identified several causal factors, the interaction between variables is often unclear. Thus, for example, while differences in technical progress between sectors may be hypothesised, the effects of this on capital and labour inputs depend on many factors including the extent of embodiment of technical progress and its 'neutrality'. *A priori* decisions on these factors are rarely possible, so that predicting the nature of the relationships between technical progress and employment is extremely difficult. These problems are in addition to the difficulties of specifying and testing the relationships between employment and various independent variables *within* a sector.

The need for a reliable data set is, of course, self-evident. The confidence with which conclusions can be drawn from statistical results must ultimately depend on the confidence one has in the accuracy of the data set. In Egypt, data on some variables which may be important in an explanation of employment growth are unavailable or unreliable. No statistics are available for capital stock disaggregated by sector, for example, and price indices for capital are unreliable. Gross investment data are published but particularly in some service sectors these are also unreliable. Thus, the results from applying a regression methodology to employment data in Section 8.2 must be treated with caution. They can offer guidance on possible causal factors in Egypt but cannot be expected to provide precise estimates or definite conclusions.

In view of the limitations of applying econometric techniques, in Section 8.3 a less rigorous methodology is adopted which nevertheless can provide insights into influences on Egypt's recent structural changes. By comparing sectoral differences in employment growth with productivity and output growth differences it is possible to confirm some of the results in Section 8.2 and identify other important factors.

To examine structural changes the sector classifications used are as discussed in Chapter 7, with a goods-producing sector being compared with a service-producing sector. There is no particular virtue in these classifications to make them superior to any others since, as Stigler noted in 1956, 'There exists no authoritative consensus on either the boundaries or the classification of the service industries' (p. 47). Insofar as theory has identified certain characteristics of 'goods' as opposed to 'services' this division of activities may be more useful. However, the primary objective of this part of the study is to include all sub-sectors in the examination so that the overall pattern of employment change can be investigated. Where appropriate individual sub-sectors are considered separately and in any case the non-agricultural goods sector (goods*) and the commercial and social service sectors are also examined in conjunction with the aggregate goods and service sectors.

Before looking at causes of structural employment changes it is helpful to summarise the evidence on employment change in terms of the goods and service classifications to be used. Employment growth rates in goods and service sectors during 1947–60 and the three five-year periods 1960–75 are presented in Table 8.1 *Relative* employment growth can be seen from the ratios in Table 8.2.

Table 8.1 shows that employment in all sectors grew faster after 1960

Table 8.1   Sectoral employment growth rates 1947–75

Sector	1947–60	1960–5	1965–70	1970–5
(1) Goods (G)	0.9	4.2	2.0	1.8
(2) Goods* (G*)	2.2	8.1	3.9	4.4
(3) Services (S)	2.4	3.8	3.3	4.3
(4) Commercial Services (CS)	1.1	3.4	2.7	3.6
(5) Social Services (SS)	3.3	4.1	3.9	4.7

Source: As Table 7.2

than during 1947–60, with the goods* sector (line 2) growing particularly rapidly during 1960–5. Secondly, for commercial services the post-1960 growth rates are a new phenomenon, pre-1960 growth being just over 1 per cent per annum. For social services, although employment growth after 1960 is higher than before, the increase in growth rates is less dramatic.

The increase in the *relative* growth of service sectors during 1960–75 is clearly demonstrated in Table 8.2. Using any of the sectoral definitions there is a systematic increase in the service to goods ratio from 1960–5, to 1970–5. However, apart from the ratio in line (3) the

Table 8.2   Ratios of sectoral employment growth rates 1947–75

Ratio	1947–60	1960–5	1965–70	1970–5
(1) S/G	2.67	0.90	1.65	2.39
(2) S/G*	1.09	0.47	0.87	0.98
(3) CS/G*	0.45	0.42	0.69	0.82
(4) SS/G*	1.50	0.51	1.00	1.07

Source: Table 8.1

high ratios pertaining in 1947–60 are not achieved again till 1970–5, and even then the ratios are somewhat below the pre-1960 period. The commercial services/goods* ratio in line (3) appears to have risen considerably above that occurring prior to 1960, confirming that employment growth in commercial services has been particularly strong from 1960.

These data confirm that at least some service activities have grown rapidly since 1960 relative to both agricultural and non-agricultural goods sectors.

8.2 APPLYING REGRESSION TECHNIQUES

To try to explain this relative shift of employment into services, in this section some of the determinants discussed in Chapter 7 will be considered using annual data for the period 1960–76. It is first necessary to specify a structural employment model which identifies influences on employment in each sector. Structural changes in employment may occur because employment in each sector is affected by the *same* factors but in different ways or to differing extents, or because each sector is influenced by different factors. Thus, for example, income growth may affect employment in all sectors but to different extents because of differences in income elasticities, while (as is shown later) rural-urban migration may have important influences on employment growth in one sector but not in another. It is on the former type of factors that economic theory has had most to say while influences confined to specific sectors may often be identified from more *ad hoc* reasoning. In Section 8.2.1 below a simple model is presented which seeks to explain different levels of employment in different sectors from differences in reactions of employment to a common set of variables.

8.2.1 A simple model

If E_i is employment in sector i, Y_i is the demand for sector i's real output and W_i is the real wage rate in sector i, it may be suggested that

$$E_i = f(Y_i, W_i) \tag{8.1}$$

Thus employment is affected by the demand for the sector's output via the production function relationship (where output supplied is de-mand-determined), and by changes in the cost of the labour input. In addition Y_i is assumed to be determined by per capita income levels, that is

$$Y_i = g_i(Z) \tag{8.2}$$

where Z is per capita income. If, as has been argued, output demanded from different sectors varies with the level of income or development, (8.2) should capture this by differences in the g_i functions across sectors.

Therefore, from (8.1) and (8.2),

$$E_i = f(g_i(Z), W_i) \tag{8.3}$$

In fact various forms of the function in (8.3) have formed the basis of many 'employment function' studies particularly in developed countries. Such studies have usually sought to explain or forecast employment in an industry, or number of industries, using output and wage variables. Differences in the effects of technology across sectors are not allowed for in this model because of the difficulties of modelling these effects with any assurance of accuracy.[1] In specifying the functional forms of (8.1) to (8.3) economic theory offers little guidance except that in (8.2) if different income elasticities across sectors are hypothesised then these elasticities may be expected to vary through time, and a double-log functional form (with the implied constant elasticity) seems less plausible. However, since the period of investigation is fairly short, constant elasticities over the period could be the most appropriate.

The model was tested using ordinary least squares regression on (8.2) and (8.3) using three functional forms of each; linear, semi-log and double-log. Thus in the linear form, for example, it is hypothesised that

$$E_i = a + \beta Y_i + \gamma W_i \qquad (8.4)$$

and $Y_i = \eta + \delta Z$ \qquad (8.5)

giving a reduced form of,

$$E_i = (a + \beta\eta) + \beta\delta Z + \gamma W_i \qquad (8.6)$$

Differences in the income elasticity of demand across sectors can be found by examining the values of δ for each sector and differences in the employment–output coefficient, β, can be derived from the co-efficient on Z in (8.6). This applies likewise to the other functional forms tested. It might be expected that the dependent variables in (8.2) and (8.3) will be affected by contemporary and/or earlier values of the independent variables. Current and lagged values of Z and W_i were therefore tested.

8.2.2 Regression results

Results were obtained for four sectors: goods*, services, commercial services and social services. Some results are presented in Tables 8.3 and 8.4 and a fuller set of results can be found in Appendix 3.

Examination of the results in Appendix 3 suggests that for almost all the combinations of lagged and contemporaneous independent variables tested the linear and double-log functional forms perform similarly, though in most cases the linear form would be the preferred specification on the basis of correct coefficient signs and improved Durbin-Watson statistics. This is the case for regressions on both equations. Secondly, in almost all cases variables enter the equations with the correct sign. In regressions on (8.2) the coefficients on per capita GDP, Z, are always positive and significant. Regressions on (8.3) produce positive coefficients on per capita GDP and negative signs as predicted on average wages.

Thirdly, the results presented in Tables 8.3 and 8.4 show those

Table 8.3 Summary of regression results: employment

Dependent Variable	Constant	Z_{-1}	W_i	$W_{i,-1}$	R^2	DW
		Independent Variables				
Goods*						
EG*	−269.2	35.72		−3.56	0.90	1.32
	(−0.80)	(10.95)		(−1.79)		
†ln EG*	2.45	1.65		−0.40	0.89	1.15
	(1.96)	(10.46)		(−1.75)		
Services						
ES	160.9	58.02		−5.93	0.97	1.95
	(0.39)	(18.25)		(−2.40)		
†ln ES	4.53	1.37		−0.44	0.96	1.91
	(5.50)	(17.47)		(−2.44)		
Commercial Services						
ECS	96.76	18.99	−0.99		0.96	1.56
	(0.57)	(17.27)	(−0.91)			
†ln ECS	3.46	1.04	−0.15		0.96	1.55
	(4.85)	(17.71)	(−1.11)			
Social Services						
ESS	−329.1	37.14		−2.01	0.95	1.77
	(−1.14)	(15.05)		(−1.42)		
†ln ESS	2.70	1.53		−0.31	0.94	1.69
	(2.41)	(13.57)		(−1.38)		

†All variables are in log. form.

Notes: Z_{-1} and $W_{i,-1}$ are respectively per capita GDP, and average annual wages in each sector, lagged one period. DW = Durbin-Watson statistic. t-statistics are in parentheses. EG* = Employment in Goods*, ES = Employment in Services, etc.

Source: Appendix 3.

equations which appeared to be most correctly specified and it can be seen that for equation (8.3) (Table 8.3), lagged values of both independent variables are preferred in all sectors except commercial services, (CS). However, as shown in Appendix 3, in the CS sector the choice between current or lagged wages is not clear-cut. Regressions on equation (8.2) (Table 8.4) suggest that lagged values of Z are

Table 8.4 Summary of regression results: output

Dependent Variable	Independent Variables		R^2	DW
	Constant	Z_{-1}		
Goods*				
YG*	−637.3	21.70	0.91	1.14
	(−5.60)	(11.86)		
†ln YG*	−1.33	1.91	0.91	1.09
	(−2.06)	(12.19)		
Services				
YS	−1215.8	33.89	0.96	1.52
	(10.51)	(18.20)		
†ln YS	−2.91	2.34	0.97	1.81
	(−6.56)	(21.72)		
Commercial Services				
YCS	−289.2	10.36	0.87	1.13
	(−4.36)	(9.70)		
†ln YCS	−1.20	1.71	0.87	1.08
	(−1.65)	(9.65)		
Social Services				
YSS	−926.6	23.53	0.95	1.21
	(−10.42)	(16.45)		
†ln YSS	−5.35	2.81	0.95	1.15
	(−7.56)	(16.34)		

†All variables are in log. form.

Notes: YG* = output from goods*, YS = output from services, etc. See also notes to Table 7.3.

Source: Appendix 3.

preferred for all four sectors, though in some cases an indeterminate Durbin-Watson statistic leaves some doubt over the specification of even the 'best' equations.

Given the data base, these results are surprisingly good. There can be reasonable confidence in the variables specified in each equation, particularly the linear forms. In Table 8.3 serial correlation does not appear to be present in the equations with the possible exception of the goods* sector. The Z_{-1} variable is always significant and R^2s are high. The role of real wages in employment determination is, however, unclear. Although in most sectors the real wage variable is not significant at the 5 per cent level, t-statistics are sufficiently high and coefficient signs consistently correct, as to suggest that reductions in real wages may encourage increased employment in each sector and vice versa. However, little confidence can be placed in the parameter estimates for each sub-sector so that differences between sectors in the responsiveness of employment to wage changes cannot be reliably ascertained from these results.

Coefficient estimates for per capita income in Table 8.3 are more reliable than those for real wages. They are also highly significant though the somewhat poorer Durbin-Watson statistics may mean that an alternative specification of the equation is justified, which in turn could alter the income coefficients. Nevertheless, it can be seen in Appendix 3 that the values of the income coefficients for each sector in Table 8.3 change very little when different combinations of the independent variables are used, suggesting that these estimates are reasonably robust.

The hypothesis of differences in income elasticities across sectors can now be considered. Table 8.5 shows estimates of elasticities from the double-log form (as reported in Table 8.3) and elasticity estimates from the linear form for three years during the period studied, 1961, 1970 and 1975. At first glance it appears that service outputs possess a higher income elasticity than goods outputs, whether constant or variable elasticities are assumed. However, in the variable elasticity case it can be seen that the service elasticity is declining more rapidly than that of goods*, giving a *relative* increase in the goods* sector elasticity. When the two service sub-sectors – commercial and social services – are considered separately, the case for higher service sector elasticities is shown to be limited to social services. Commercial service elasticities are lower than goods* although they are increasing slightly relative to goods* elasticities in the variable elasticity case. Because of the measurement problems associated with social service outputs the apparent higher elasticity here must also be treated with caution. Since this sector's output is measured from wage payments, the higher 'elasticity' measure actually indicates that the change in the social service wage bill exceeds the change in goods* output for a given increase in per capita incomes. To the extent that a rise in these social service 'costs' represent increased 'value' of social service output as a response to increased demand, social services may be

Table 8.5 Estimates of income elasticities and employment-output coefficients

Sector	Constant Elasticities (log-log regression)	Declining Elasticities			Employment-Output Coefficients	
		1961	1970	1975	log-log regression	linear regression
Goods*	1.91	2.34	1.87	1.58	0.864	1.646
Services	2.34	3.33	2.31	1.81	0.585	1.712
Commercial Services	1.71	2.19	1.79	1.53	0.608	1.833
Social Services	2.81	4.30	2.65	1.96	0.544	1.578

Source: Appendix 3

considered to possess higher elasticities. However, as shown later, further evidence on the growth of Egypt's social services would suggest that, in general, this is not the case.

Despite the apparently higher elasticities for service outputs (and social service outpts), the regressions in Table 8.3 indicate that the overall effect of increases in per capita income on sectoral employment is, in some cases, less in service sectors than in goods.* The income coefficient on lnECS, for example, is 1.04 as against 1.65 for goods.* (ln EG*.) This must arise because of lower values for the employment-output coefficient (β in equation (8.4)) in services. Estimates of these coefficients, which represent the technical relationship between output and employment derived from the production function in each sector, are also presented in Table 8.5. The estimates from the log-regressions indicate that for a given increase in output within a sector more additional employment will be generated in the goods* sector than in either of the service sub-sectors, (and therefore in total services also). However β values estimated from linear regressions suggest a higher value for commercial services than goods*. Therefore the employment-output coefficient in social services would appear to be unambiguously lower than goods* while that for commercial services (if linear results are adopted) is probably higher.

If, as has often been argued, service activities are more labour-intensive than goods production, a higher value of β is to be expected in services, increases in output requiring more additional labour input than in goods sectors. The lower coefficient estimates for social services (and possibly commercial services) are therefore unexpected. The most plausible explanation probably lies in the output measure. If output increases estimated for the goods* sector represent genuine improvements in real output, significant employment increases may be expected. If, in social services on the other hand, output increases represent mainly *average* wage rises, 'output' will rise with little employment change. It would seem, therefore, that although employment in each of the sectors considered can be explained fairly well within the model used, there does not appear to be a consistent pattern of higher income elasticities or higher employment-output coefficients in service sectors than in goods* sectors.

Finally, since the data in Section 8.1 suggested that not only is service employment increasing relative to goods employment but the relative *rate of growth* of service employment is increasing, it is interesting to examine the effects of *changes* in income and wages on the *change* in employment in each sector. It may be, for example, that while employment does not react to changes in wage rates, the rate of change of wages does affect the rate of employment growth. Regression results for these difference equations, in linear and double-log form, are given in Appendix 3.[2] They suggest that, in general, changes in employment are not strongly influenced by changes in per capita incomes or wages, in any of the four sectors. Wage rate changes have most effect in social services but in commercial services and goods* sectors wage coefficients are insignificant and sometimes wrongly signed. Income changes similarly perform poorly and R^2s are generally low. It seems clear that, at least for the 1960–76 period as a whole, faster employment growth in services cannot be explained with reference to growth rates of income or average wages.

8.3 DIFFERENCES IN OUTPUT AND PRODUCTIVITY

The evidence considered in Section 8.1 suggested that there were differences within the 1960–75 period in the growth rates of goods and service sectors. This may reflect differences within the period in the factors influencing structural change. Unfortunately, because of the limited number of observations it is not possible to examine subperiods using the regression methodology. Also, differences between sectors in the rates of growth of productivity were not examined in Section 8.2.[3]

In this section, therefore, a less rigorous, but nevertheless, useful, methodology is used to help identify influences on service and goods employment growth and possible differences between the sub-periods previously discussed.

8.3.1 The method of analysis

The method adopted here, first used by Fuchs (1965) for the USA, consists of examining the association of employment growth rates with output and productivity growth rates. It can be shown that for any sector these variables are linked identically such that,

$$\dot{E}_s - \dot{E}_g \equiv (\dot{Q}_s - \dot{Q}_g) - (\dot{P}_s - \dot{P}_g) \tag{8.7}$$

where $\dot{E}$, $\dot{Q}$ and $\dot{P}$ are the proportionate rates of growth of employment output and productivity (as measured by output per man) respectively and subscripts g and s refer to the goods and service sectors respectively. From (8.7) it can be seen that sectoral differences in employment growth must be equal to the difference between sectoral differentials in output and productivity growth. If output and productivity are exogenous (see below) then, '*other things being equal*, a more rapid rise in real output for the service sector compared with the goods sector would imply a more elastic demand for services' (Fuchs, 1965, p. 8).

Thus, although the hypothesis that faster employment growth in services relative to goods is due to higher income elasticities for services is not tested directly, the association of a given value of $(\dot{E}_s - \dot{E}_g)$ with a similar value of $(\dot{Q}_s - \dot{Q}_g)$ could be interpreted as indicating a higher income elasticity in aggregate for services. Alternatively, if a positive employment growth differential appears to be associated with a similar negative productivity growth differential, the hypothesis that slower productivity growth in services accounts for its relative employment growth becomes more plausible.

The relationship between growth rates in the three variables will be examined for the three sub-periods discussed earlier, namely 1960–5, 1965–70 and 1970–5. Differences in the relative employment growth rates between these periods are sufficiently large as to suggest that factors affecting employment growth may not be the same in all periods.

A number of methodological problems arise from the identity between employment, output and productivity growth discussed above. If, within the identity, output and productivity are to be held to exert influences on employment, both output and productivity variables must be exogenously given, and *behaviourally* independent.[4] In fact, there are likely to be causal relationships between output and productivity. Different rates of productivity growth between sectors, for example, may be expected to affect relative prices which in turn, via demand changes, can affect sectoral output growth rates. Conversely the Ver Doorn law suggests that higher rates of output growth may be expected to encourage faster rates of growth in employment *and* productivity, through economies of scale and the encouragement of faster technical progress. In practice in studies of employment change (e.g. Fuchs, 1965) it is typically assumed that the effects of interdependencies between output and productivity growth are sufficiently small as to allow the two variables to be treated as independent.

In mainly market economies it is probably not unreasonable to assume that in general output and productivity growth variables in equation (8.7) are exogenous. Thus employment growth is determined by the rate of output growth (usually assumed to be demand-determined) and the rate of productivity growth. However, in economies where the government is heavily involved in the production of marketed goods and services, particularly in developing countries with high unemployment, it may adopt employment-creating policies which affect output and productivity. In Egypt, for example, it has been suggested that productivity fell or grew slowly in some industries in the early 1960s because the government's 'employment drive' in this period expanded employment beyond that required for production. Similarly it is likely that there were times during the 1960–75 period when output was constrained by supply factors despite growing demand. Balance of payments deficits in the 1960s led to brief but severe import restrictions in some years which prevented some industries from producing at full capacity due to shortages of foreign input goods.

While these factors undoubtedly did affect the relationship between output, productivity and employment in some parts of the economy during this period, overall the effects were probably small and short-lived. For the goods and service sectors as a whole, over the 1960–75 period, it is probably reasonable to regard output as demand-determined and output and productivity as exogenous. However, in interpreting the data later in this chapter it is important to be aware of possible violations of these assumptions.

To estimate output differences between sectors two measures of real output are used – Gross Domestic Product at constant 1960 prices (measure I), and at current prices (measure II). It is likely that implicit price deflators for services (and particularly social services) are underestimates relative to goods so that the constant price data probably overestimates the output differential in favour of services. Conversely, current price data which assume both sectors' prices increase at the same rate probably underestimate the real growth in service output relative to goods. It is, however, likely that measure II (current prices) is the more accurate for this comparison.[5]

A preliminary examination of the association of employment growth differences between sectors with differences in output and productivity growth showed that this association was variable across time periods, and sensitive to the sub-sectors included. That is, the variability in output and productivity growth differentials was sufficiently large as to confirm that neither higher income elasticities for, or slower productivity growth in, services could be supported overall. The results (available in Gemmell, 1985) therefore suggested the need for a more disaggregated study of sector differentials to explain relative service employment growth. This is pursued in the remainder of this chapter, considering first commercial services (8.3.2) and then social services (8.3.3).

8.3.2 Commercial services

The commercial services sector is composed of two sub-sectors for which separate data are available: finance and internal trade (of which, in employment terms, wholesale and retail trade constituted 96 per cent in 1960) and transport and communications (of which, in employment terms, road and rail transport constituted 67 per cent in 1960).

Data for employment, output and productivity growth in these sectors are presented in Tables 8.6 and 8.7 and it is clear that the trends in these variables over the 1960–75 period are quite different across sectors.

Both transport and communications, and finance and trade sectors show increases in employment growth relative to both goods sectors from 1960–5 to 1970–5. However, whereas in finance and trade this is a smooth increase over the three periods, in transport and communications a large increase in relative rates of employment growth occurs in 1965–70 which decreases again in 1970–5 though relative employment growth remains considerably above that of the first five years. Also, compared to the goods sector, employment growth in transport and communications is higher in all three periods, but for finance and trade this only occurs in 1970–5.

Differences in output and productivity growth trends are also evident. For transport and communications the figures suggest that both output and productivity growth rates were much slower than in goods (or goods*) during 1965–70, having grown substantially faster for the previous five years. 1970–5 sees a return towards the earlier position of output and productivity growing faster relative to goods* (though less markedly when agriculture is included), but somewhat less than the differentials were during 1960–5. For finance and trade, however, Table 8.6 shows that the acceleration in employment growth relative to the goods* (and goods) sectors is associated unambiguously with increasing output and productivity differentials.

Transport and Communications: The rapid decline of output and output per man in transport and communications during 1965–70 is almost entirely due to the cessation of the flow of revenues from the Suez Canal as a result of the June 1967 war with Israel, when the loss of

Table 8.6 Employment, output and productivity growth differentials in transport and communications (T&C) and goods sectors, 1960–75

		1960–65			1965–70			1970–75		
		$(\dot{E}_s - \dot{E}_g)$	$(\dot{Q}_s - \dot{Q}_g)$	$(\dot{P}_s - \dot{P}_g)$	$(\dot{E}_s - \dot{E}_g)$	$(\dot{Q}_s - \dot{Q}_g)$	$(\dot{P}_s - \dot{P}_g)$	$(\dot{E}_s - \dot{E}_g)$	$(\dot{Q}_s - \dot{Q}_g)$	$(\dot{P}_s - \dot{P}_g)$
(T & C) – Goods	I	0.7	5.2	4.3	2.6	–8.5	–11.0	1.3	9.1	7.5
	II		5.0	4.2		–10.7	–13.2		–0.9	–2.2
(T & C) – Goods*	I	–3.2	2.8	5.7	0.7	–9.6	–10.3	–1.3	7.6	8.6
	II		4.0	7.0		–10.8	–11.5		–0.4	0.8

Table 8.7 Employment, output and productivity growth differentials in finance and trade (F & I) and goods sectors, 1960–75

		1960–65			1965–70			1970–75		
		$(\dot{E}_s - \dot{E}_g)$	$(\dot{Q}_s - \dot{Q}_g)$	$(\dot{P}_s - \dot{P}_g)$	$(\dot{E}_s - \dot{E}_g)$	$(\dot{Q}_s - \dot{Q}_g)$	$(\dot{P}_s - \dot{P}_g)$	$(\dot{E}_s - \dot{E}_g)$	$(\dot{Q}_s - \dot{Q}_g)$	$(\dot{P}_s - \dot{P}_g)$
(F & I) – Goods	I		−2.7	−1.2		1.0	1.2		7.1	4.8
		−1.4			−0.1			2.0		
	II		−3.2	−1.6		0.4	0.5		6.3	4.1
(F & I) – Goods*	I		−5.1	0.2		−0.1	1.9		5.6	5.9
		−5.3			−2.0			−0.6		
	II		−4.2	−1.2		0.3	2.2		6.8	7.1

Note: Average annual rates of growth are reported; thus $(\dot{E}_s - \dot{E}_g) \approx (\dot{Q}_s - \dot{Q}_g) - (\dot{P}_s - \dot{P}_g)$
  I = Valued at constant (1960) prices; II = Valued at current prices.

Source: Calculated from data in CAPMAS, *Statistical Yearbook of the UAR*, Cairo, various issues.

the Sinai peninsula forced the prolonged closure of the canal. The size of the Suez Canal 'industry' was very small in employment terms (under 4 per cent of transport and communications sector employment in 1965), but it contributed about 50 per cent of total value added in the transport and communications sector in 1965. The effect of the war, therefore, was to drastically reduce value added but with little effect on employment growth in the transport and communications sector as a whole. Thus, the apparent fall in output per man can hardly have been the cause of the relative employment growth in this service sector since productivity fell in a different part of the sector from that which contributed most to employment growth.

Output and productivity differentials recovered during the 1970–5 period but if, as previously suggested, measure II is the more accurate, this still represents a fall compared with the first half of the 1960s. Thus, although service output growth declined relative to goods after 1965, relative employment growth increased with an even larger fall in relative productivity growth. It would seem, therefore, that the transport and communications sector partially recovered after the 1967 war, despite the continuing loss of canal revenues, because of the growth of internal transportation and communications facilities. However, relative output growth is still slow compared to the early 1960s (using measure II), and this would seem to be the result of at least three factors.

Firstly, the continued loss of canal revenues, plus the effects of the 1973 war, served to reduce the growth in output, but without similar effects on the sector's employment.

Secondly, the growth in employment in the transport and communications sector has undoubtedly been affected by the expansion of Egypt's urban 'informal' sector over the period, encouraged by the lack of job opportunities in the non-agricultural goods sector. This growth of the informal sector will be discussed in more detail later, but it is sufficient to point out here that in the *transport* sector the expansion of employment through informal activities may have added little to output so helping to explain the slow productivity growth. Mongi and Hanafi have pointed to the importance of disguised unemployment in the form of 'followers' – people who accompany transportation wagons, helping in loading and unloading' (Hanafi and Mongi, 1975, p. 299). In production terms, these people are superfluous to needs, but are able to maintain their jobs because of public sector employment policy.

Thirdly, a lack of adequate capital replacement and modernisation in the transport and communications sector has probably hindered output growth. Losses of road and rail equipment such as buses and carriages through wars, internal violence and general wear and tear have often not been made good because of higher priorities (rightly or wrongly) for limited government finance, or foreign exchange constraints prohibiting importation of the necessary equipment.

These three factors would explain why employment continued to grow in transport and communications despite limited output growth, exceeding that of goods sector employment because of the growth of 'informal' activities, particularly in the 1970s, which beset the transport and communications sector (both public and private) more than goods.

Finance and Trade: It was noted earlier that in contrast to transport and communications, relative employment growth in finance and trade after 1965 was associated with faster productivity and output growth. This has occurred for various reasons. Firstly, the trade sector, along with agriculture, was one of the sectors least affected by the 1967 war so that output growth fell less during 1965–70 than was the case in the goods-producing sectors. This was partly a direct consequence of the relative output growth in agriculture, since wholesale and retail trade acts as much as an outlet for agricultural as for industrial commodities. However, during the 1970s when almost all sectors experienced faster rates of output growth, the finance and trade sector also experienced a relative output growth compared with the goods sectors, suggesting that the overall post-1965 growth in this sector is more than a phenomenon created by the war.

The trade sector has experienced a growing demand for consumer goods to which it has been more able to respond. A rapidly growing population and the expansion of agricultural output, and imports, to meet their needs, have increased output and employment in retail trade. In addition the growing demand in Egypt over the period, noted by various commentators, for western luxury consumer goods, has also had an expansionary effect on retail trade. The main streets of Cairo and Alexandria increasingly house retail outlets selling modern manufactured consumer goods, often imported, for the increasing numbers of middle-income consumers in Egypt. This increase in employment may, therefore, actually have been *caused* by output growth.

Thirdly, increases in informal activities have taken place perhaps mostly in the retail trade sector, so increasing employment disproportionately. This would not have the effect of reducing productivity to the extent that it did in transport and communications because the majority of informal activities in this sector are private, often self-employed, and those which can be captured by statistics are likely to be more profit orientated. For example, a casual worker employed to unload wagons in the public transport sector will be paid regardless of output, whereas the private trader's income is dependent on sales. There is, of course, a growing number of publicly-owned department stores in retail trade, which it is sometimes argued, suffer from overmanning as do other public services. It is quite possible, however, that where these department stores substitute for small private traders, they may still be more efficient, with greater potential for increasing value added by aiming at Egypt's growing middle-classes.

Finally, the relative increase in finance and trade sector employment would seem to be co-existent with rising output and productivity growth partly because of the increasing contribution, in terms of value added, of banking and insurance services. In 1965 banking and insurance formed only 5 per cent of finance and trade employment but contributed 12 per cent to value added in the sector. These services have developed since 1965 under government policy and, being fairly capital-intensive (relative to the rest of finance and trade sector), have added more to output than employment, increasing the rate of output growth associated with employment growth in the finance and trade sector as a whole. The expansion in financial services is almost certainly related to Egypt's increasing openness to western banking interests, and to the demise of Beirut as the Middle East's major financial centre.

Informal Services: So far it has been argued that the growth in 'informal' activities in Egypt since the mid-1960s is partly responsible for the increase in the relative growth in employment in commercial services and this can represent either productive employment or disguised unemployment.

Mabro (1974) has suggested that a problem of disguised unemployment was evident in Egypt's service sector before 1960, and there can be little doubt that it has also played an important part in the expansion of trade and transport services since then. However, the development of some informal services certainly results from an effective demand for them and not simply as a product of excess labour supply. Bauer and Yamey's observation that demand for transport and trade services may grow is certainly relevant in Egypt. They suggest that lack of storage space for poor producers and consumers means that

they may require the services of small-scale traders to collect small lots of farm produce at frequent intervals. Among large sections of the population there may have to be a number of traders catering for their needs by dealing in small quantities (Bauer and Yamey, 1957, p. 39).

In Egypt the informal sector has arisen firstly, because population growth in urban and rural areas has exceeded the growth in modern sector employment opportunities, and secondly, because many rural-urban migrants do not have the appropriate skills for the modern sector.

It seems that the gap between population growth and modern sector jobs widened from the mid-1960s and migration increased. Some evidence of this can be found in Table 8.8 which shows changes in employment and urban population between 1960, 1966 and 1976 (the population census years). The average annual increases in employment in the goods* sector (which is almost entirely 'modern' and urban) were substantially lower in the second period, while over the same periods the urban population increase rose slightly from an annual average of about 161 000 to 166 000.[6] Transport and communications employment increases also show a slowdown but in finance and trade where the private informal sector is more strongly represented, annual employment increases were about 35 per cent higher in 1966–76 than they had been during 1960–6.

Between 1966 and 1976, the *rate* of growth of Cairo's labour force (and that of the other urban governates) may have been declining but absolute numbers of new entrants were still rising. It is inevitable then, with the goods* sector failing to expand adequately that much of the excess labour supply would find ways into the informal sector and it

Table 8.8   Average annual increases in employment and urban population 1960–66 and 1966–76 (thousands)

	Urban population	Goods* employment	Commercial service employment		
			T&C	F&I	TOTAL
(1) Annual Average 1960–66	161.7	71.4	14.9	19.5	34.3
(2) Annual Average 1966–76	166.2	65.3	11.4	26.4	37.8
(3) Ratio (2):(1)	1.03	0.91	0.74	1.35	1.10

Source: As Table 8.7

does seem that employment statistics in commercial services have captured some of this increase.

8.3.3 Social services

Because of limited disaggregation of available employment data, this sector includes a proportion of private 'personal' services such as restaurants, tailors, etc. (which would be more appropriately classified with commercial services), and social services (education, health, recreation, administration, etc.) 87 per cent of which, in employment terms, were publicly owned in 1960. This data deficiency makes it difficult to assess trends in each of these two services over the whole 1960–75 period. However, it can be ascertained that the contribution of private services (which are mostly personal) to value added in the total social service sector fell from 42 per cent in 1960 to 33 per cent in 1965, but only by a further 1 percentage point to 32 per cent over the nine years to 1974.[7] Employment data show a similar pattern to that of value added between 1960 and 1965 and if this continued even approximately after 1965 then the share of private in total social services probably fell very little after that date. In terms of actual numbers employed this implies that the fairly static employment levels in private social services between 1960 and 1965 began to increase at a rate not much less than that of public social services after 1965. That is, the relative growth of social service employment was both a private and a public phenomenon. Indeed it does seem that the static employment *level* and declining *share* of service employment experienced by private social services during 1960–5 was peculiar to this period while both prior and subsequent to it, employment was growing faster than in the goods sector. Mead (1967) notes the large employment increase between 1947 and 1960 in 'personal services not elsewhere classified' (corresponding to the 'personal services' category here) which he considers to be 'a clear case of the spread of agricultural underemployment into the services' (Mead, 1967, p. 153), that is, the informal sector.

Turning to the causes of social service growth evident in available employment statistics, Table 8.9 presents estimates of employment, output and output per man growth differentials between social services and both goods sectors. It would, of course, be false to think that changes in relative output or productivity could *explain* employment

Table 8.9 Employment, output and productivity growth differentials in social services and goods sectors, 1960–75

		1960–65			1965–70			1970–75	
	$(\dot{E}_s - \dot{E}_g)$	$(\dot{Q}_s - \dot{Q}_g)$	$(\dot{P}_s - \dot{P}_g)$	$(\dot{E}_s - \dot{E}_g)$	$(\dot{Q}_s - \dot{Q}_g)$	$(\dot{P}_s - \dot{P}_g)$	$(\dot{E}_s - \dot{E}_g)$	$(\dot{Q}_s - \dot{Q}_g)$	$(\dot{P}_s - \dot{P}_g)$
SS – Goods I	-0.1	1.9	1.9	1.9	2.7	0.8	2.9	5.6	2.5
II		0.7	0.8		1.1	-0.8		2.1	-0.8
SS – Goods* I	-4.0	-0.5	3.3	0.0	1.6	1.5	-0.3	4.1	3.6
II		-0.3	3.6		1.0	0.9		2.6	2.2

Note: The slight fall in the employment differential (SS–Goods*) during 1970–75 arises mainly because of the effects of a large rise in construction employment during 1975. For the rest of the period $\dot{E}_s$ exceeded $\dot{E}_g$.

Source: As Table 8.7

growth in this sector because of the way in which GDP is calculated for public social services. Rising GDP in government administration, for example, is particularly difficult to interpret. However, the figures do provide some insights into the underlying influences on social service employment growth.

It would seem from the table that the relative employment growth is primarily associated with a relative decline in productivity in 1965–70 and a relative rise in output in 1970–5 (using current price data). For example, comparing social services with the total goods sector, measure II shows that the 2 percentage point rise in the employment differential (from −0.1 per cent to 1.9 per cent) between 1960–65 and 1965–70 is associated with only a 0.4 percentage point rise in the output differential, but a 1.6 percentage point fall in the output per man differential. A further 1 percentage point rise in the employment differential in 1970–75 occurs with a 1 percentage point rise in the output differential (from 1.1 per cent to 2.1 per cent) with the productivity differential remaining constant at −0.8 per cent.

This association of relative employment growth with a relative productivity decline may help to explain the nature of the employment growth experienced by social services. Firstly, as previously noted the sharp decline in the private sector's share of total social services during 1960–65 had been much reduced after 1965 which represented a rise in enumerated employment in this sector. Since this private sector, producing mostly personal services, is less productive than the public social service sector (in terms of GDP per head), this would serve to reduce recorded productivity growth experienced by the social service sector as a whole.

Secondly, it is likely that much of the employment increase in the public sector was in the form of low wage employment (and therefore lower GPD-creating employment) which would reduce the rate of productivity growth relative to employment. Between 1960 and 1965 employment in government administration grew faster than any other major public social service sub-sector, followed by health services. While the growth in health services is a valuable achievement in a country with poor health facilities and rapid population growth, it is unlikely that the growth in employment in Egypt's already large bureaucracy was matched by a similar growth in real output. Hanafi and Mongi (1975) point out that this increase in employment, amounting to an average of 21 per cent per annum over the five year period, was associated with an average increase in total real wages in the sector of only 12 per cent per annum. This cannot be entirely explained by a failure of money wages to keep pace with inflation, but they suggest, 'may be due to either employing a considerable number of unskilled labour or to the increase of young workers with relatively moderate start wages, or due to both reasons together' (p. 286). Without more detailed information on the development of employment in government administration, we cannot be sure that this is the cause, nor whether this trend continued after 1965. The relative decline in social service productivity to 1970 would certainly be consistent with this. By the same reasoning, however, the rise in output and (possibly) productivity differentials after 1970 is not consistent with low-wage employment expansion. Two factors may account for this rise after 1970. Either a larger expansion in high-wage employment which gives the appearance of faster productivity growth may have occurred after 1970, or if the share of government administration in total social service output fell, to be replaced, say, by private services, then the influence of wages in government administration would be less evident in social service output and productivity movements. In fact, as will be shown, there is evidence that both these factors are likely to have operated during the early 1970s. Firstly, however, causes of the expansion of Egypt's *public* social services sector, will be considered.

Public Social Services: The causes of expansion in this sector can perhaps best be summarised in two categories – public employment policies and policies towards education and social services.

The cornerstone of the government's *employment policy* in the early 1960s was to reduce hours worked per man in the public sectors of the economy and increase their employment levels so that hopefully costs would remain steady but unemployment would fall. This was the reasoning behind the employment drive begun in 1961 causing manufacturing industry and government administration particularly to increase their labour forces significantly after that date. Unfortunately, opportunities to reduce hours worked per man by banning overtime had little effect in government administration where there is little use of overtime, and in manufacturing, as Mabro and Radwan discovered, unofficial ways to compensate workers for lost earnings were discovered, until eventually rigidities created by the ban were sufficient to force the government to remove it. At the same time, legislation preventing the sacking of employees meant that new employees absorbed into the public bureaucracy, most of whom (if not all) were not needed, became a permanent burden on public finance. The aim of this arm of policy was to solve much of the mass unemployment problem and thus resulted in increased absorption of unskilled, low-wage labour. Government administration was particularly susceptible to this type of employment creation.

The government's *policy towards education* has also had a significant impact on the growth in the bureaucracy. The government has been committed since the 1961/2 Socialist Laws to employ all graduates, should they wish it, in the public sector and the rapid growth in the number of graduates seeking jobs as a result of the expansion in the education facilities in Egypt, particularly since the early 1960s, has meant an increasing flow into the Civil Service. After 1965 the scarcity of goods* sector jobs, both private and public seems to have led to an even greater proportion of graduates being employed in government administration.

In many cases a Civil Service job may be the easiest option for a graduate. Berger (1954) found after surveying 249 senior officials in the Civil Service, that the majority had entered because of a lack of other job opportunities, and that the younger civil servants interviewed in particular had considered other careers more seriously. This occurred despite the fact that nearly 80 per cent of those interviewed found only a 'low' level of satisfaction from the job. Therefore it would seem that most graduates who enter the civil service do so, not necessarily because they are attracted by the work, but because there are few other opportunities for them, and those 'other opportunities' as shown earlier, were less from the mid-1960s onwards.

Figures for the number of students graduating from universities over the 1960–75 period provide some insights into the pattern of government administration employment growth. These are presented in Figure 8.1. Government administration tends to employ graduates from the humanities faculty rather than the science faculty since the latter have less difficulty in obtaining jobs in other sectors of the economy. Figure 8.1 indicates that science graduates increased at a fairly steady rate over the period, while humanities graduates increased particularly rapidly between 1962 and 1967, and after 1972. The period from 1967 to 1972 on the other hand, experienced a relatively static annual level of humanities graduates. It is interesting to note that the available data on employment in government administration from 1960–5 show that absorption increased considerably from 1963, that is, the years when graduates in humanities also increased most rapidly. Some of the employment increase is, of course, due to the employment drive. From the graduates figures then, it could be expected, *ceteris paribus*, that the proportion of graduates among new employees in

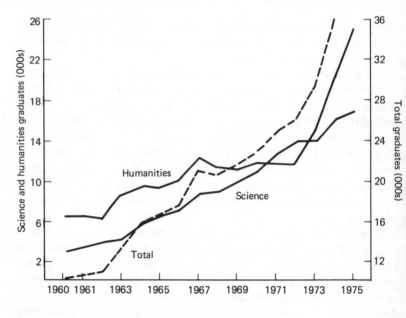

Figure 8.1   Graduates from Egyptian universities 1960–75

Source: As Table 8.7

government administration would be greater during 1962–67 and 1972–5 and less during 1967–72. Since graduates have a much higher average wage in government employment this will tend to increase the average wage for the sector as a whole during the former two periods, and reduce it in the latter. With output data for government administration reflecting data on total wages very closely, this may help to explain why the employment growth in the social service sector was associated with a relative productivity and output rise during the early 1970s.

Finally, there is some evidence that health and education services which are almost entirely publicly-owned, have contributed to the relative employment growth in social services over the 1960–75 period. Employment data are incomplete but it is known that the numbers of 'physicians, dentists and pharmacists' for example, grew faster after 1975 than before, causing the decline in the population per physician ratio to proceed after 1965 at a pace almost twice as fast as the 1960–5 rate.

In education, trends are not so clear-cut. Total teaching staff increased by an average of about 6 per cent per annum during 1960–5 but only by 3 per cent per annum thereafter. This decline is much less than the decline in employment growth in the goods sector. However, teaching staff formed only about 55 per cent of total education sector employment in 1960 with teaching staff growing slightly slower than other categories during the 1960–5 period. Thus, growth rates in teaching staff both before and after 1965 may not give an accurate picture of the growth in education employment overall.

Private Services: Earlier it was argued that the association of faster employment growth in social service sector after 1970 with faster output and productivity growth, could occur if the share of the public social service sector was falling in favour of a larger private sector, and if this private sector was experiencing faster output and productivity growth.

It was also noted earlier that the share of the public sector in social service value added fell from 42 per cent in 1960 to 33 per cent in 1965, but probably only about a further 1 per cent to 32 per cent by 1974. Thus the influences of public sector output and productivity trends on the social service sector as a whole would be very much less in 1965–75 than they were during 1960–5. This is confirmed by comparing various government social service expenditures (which obviously must be closely related to public social service GDP) to the total social service sector GDP, which suggests an increasing share of the public sector in social service output 1960–5 but a considerable reversal in the trend after 1965. This, of course, does not confirm that faster output and productivity growth after 1970 was due to a greater influence of an expanding private sector, unless the private sector also experienced rising output and productivity growth. Some evidence on this can be obtained by pooling data from different employment and output sources in Table 8.10. The 1965–76 period is not strictly comparable with the earlier period but the results are in line with what would be expected and confirm the suggestion that after 1965 the relative decline of private 'social' service employment was reversed and in particular, rates of output and productivity growth were much larger in the later period.

Table 8.10   Output, employment and productivity growth in private social services

Period	Employment Growth	Average Annual Rates of: Output Growth	Productivity Growth
1960–65	0.1	2.8	2.7
1965–76	2.4*	7.3†	4.8

†1976 data are obtained by mulitiplying the proportion of value added produced privately in social services in 1974 (0.318), with total social service GDP in 1976.
*Figures for public social services in 1976 were calculated from Survey of Employment in Government and Public Services in February 1977 by the Central Agency for Organisation and Administration (CAOA). This was subtracted from annual data on employment in (total) social services in December 1976.

Source: CAPMAS, *Statistical Yearbook of the UAR*, Cairo, various issues; CAOA, *Survey of Employment in Government and Public Service*, Cairo, 1977; and National Bank of Egypt, *Economic Bulletin*, 1975, 4.

8.4   RELATIVE OUTPUT PRICES

The use of output and productivity differentials in the previous section involved two measures of real output each based on different assumptions regarding the movements of relative output prices. Of course, as argued in Chapter 7, changes in the relative rates of real output growth across sectors may actually result from inter-sectoral relative price changes. As noted earlier data on sectoral price levels over the 1960–75 period in Egypt are not thought to be very reliable which makes the data unsuited for rigorous analysis. However, bearing in mind possible inaccuracies, it is interesting to examine the hypothesis that relative service employment growth was influenced by a relative decline in the price of service outputs stimulating increased demand for services.

Although it has not been possible to confirm higher income elasticities for services, the evidence of the previous section certainly suggested strong demand for some services. Also in *each* of the three service sub-sectors (transport and communications, finance and trade and social services) the rising employment differential in favour of services was associated with a rising real output differential in all the periods examined, with the exception of the unusual changes in transport and communications in 1965–70 (see Tables 8.6, 8.7 and 8.9). It is interest-ing, therefore, to examine whether this relative rise in real service output is associated with a fall in relative service prices. Table 8.11 presents data on ratios of price indices for the goods and service sectors examined above, calculated from deflators implicit in official GDP estimates.[9] These figures should be treated with caution especially since social service deflators are probably underestimated. At first sight there appears to be some support for the hypothesis, with each service/goods ratio showing a systematic decline over the three five-year periods. Prices in transport and communications relative to goods, for example, in 1975 are almost half what they were in 1960. The decline in each ratio is especially large during 1970–75. However, examining service/goods* ratios reveals *rising* relative service prices to 1965, which generally either rise further thereafter or at least remain above 1960 levels. What is clear is that relatively large rises in agricultural prices are not matched by non-agricultural goods price rises. From 1960 to 1970, goods* sector prices have risen similarly to prices in transport and communications and social services. However, after 1970 goods* sector prices appear to have risen faster than in these two service categories. Finance and trade prices seem to have risen consistently faster than goods* prices.

Table 8.11   Ratios of price indices for goods and service sectors, 1960–75

Sector	1960	1965	1970	1975
(T&C)/Goods	1.0	0.988	0.897	0.566
(F & I(/Goods	1.0	0.978	0.947	0.897
SS/Goods	1.0	0.944	0.874	0.741
(T & C)/Goods*	1.0	1.055	1.006	0.696
(F & I)/Goods*	1.0	1.044	1.062	1.103
SS/Goods*	1.0	1.008	0.982	0.911

Source: As Table 8.7, and calculated from World Bank data subsequently published in Ikram (1980).

Therefore, it seems safe to conclude that, even if price rises in services in general, or social services in particular, are underestimated, there is little support for the hypothesis that relative service output growth was encouraged by a relative price fall. Output differentials increased in favour of services relative to *both* the goods and goods* sectors but the only sizeable relative price change occurred between agriculture on the one hand and services and goods* on the other. At best, relative price falls in services could only help to explain some relative employment growth in 1970–75. Underestimates of service sector deflators is, however, also more likely in this period which witnessed generally higher inflation.

8.5 SUMMARY AND CONCLUSIONS

Following more extensive evidence in Chapter 7, it was shown in Section 8.1 that over the 1960–75 period there was a strong trend towards increasing employment in service activities, both commercial and social as opposed to goods-producing activities. In some services this appeared to be a return to trends evident prior to 1960 but which had been halted in the early 1960s, while in others the strong absolute and relative employment growth was a new phenomenon.

Using a simple model in Section 8.2 in which changes in per capita income and average wages were hypothesised to affect employment, data for 1960–76 were tested using regression analysis. Although wages did not seem to be important in employment determination, per capita income effects were generally strong. However, the hypothesis that sectoral employment differences were affected by differences in income elasticities across sectors did not find much support.

In Section 8.3 the respective influences of output and productivity on employment growth were considered for three five-year periods, and it was shown that neither one of these factors was dominant overall. The association of relative employment growth with changes in relative output and productivity growth was different across periods and types of service. Demand for some services, however, did appear to be strong.

Considering commercial and social services separately, it was argued that in both categories there was evidence of a relative growth in private 'informal' activities and public sector expansion from the mid-1960s. (The growth in private 'social' services was, however, mainly because limited data disaggregation did not allow these services to be classified with commercial services, which would have been more appropriate.)

In the commercial services sector, transport and communication services appear to have grown in association with declining productivity growth mainly because of disguised unemployment in the public sector and the disproportionate effects of the 1967 war. Slower productivity growth could hardly, therefore, be interpreted as *causing* faster employment growth in this case. Finance and trade on the other hand experienced rising output and productivity growth, relative to goods sectors over the period, which probably stems from the growing urban demand for agricultural and luxury goods which has boosted wholesale and retail trade services. These have been mostly private, though the public sector has probably also benefited here.

The employment growth experienced by social services has also been a private and public phenomenon. Public services, as expected, are by far the larger in this sector and it was shown that administration and health services have been among the fastest growing. The available evidence suggests that, at least in administration, much of this increase represents disguised unemployment arising from excessive graduate employment under Egypt's education policies; and sizeable increases in low-wage labour as part of social welfare policy. Part of the expansion, however, has undoubtedly been a consequence of the governments' social goals of expanding health and education facilities to the majority of the population.

Finally, it was noted that trends evident during 1965–70 were strongly influenced by selective effects of the 1967 war which had a large effect on commercial service sector output in particular, mainly as a result of the closure of the Suez canal. Because of the low labour intensity of services associated with the Suez canal, there was little effect on employment in this sector.

9 The Role of the Non-market Sector in Egypt

9.1 INTRODUCTION

It was argued in Chapter 3 that a sizeable relative growth in an economy's non-market sector may be expected, in some circumstances, to be associated with macroeconomic problems such as balance of payments deficits or high inflation rates. Such problems have been evident in Egypt since the early 1960s and in this chapter the marketed/non-marketed distinction is applied to the Egyptian economy in an attempt to help to explain these problems. First some effects of interaction between the market and non-market sectors on productivity growth are considered, and in Section 9.3 these interactions are examined in the context of the Egyptian economy over the period 1960–76. Following consideration of the effects on output, employment and prices in Sections 9.4 and 9.5, Section 9.6 discusses some of the causes of non-market growth in Egypt.

9.2 THE NON-MARKET SECTOR AND PRODUCTIVITY GROWTH

The market sector was defined in Chapter 3 as the aggregate of all sectors producing outputs which are sold 'in the market place'. This includes all industrial and non-industrial goods whether produced under private or public ownership, and all services which are sold such as banking, insurance and distribution. The non-market sector includes all outputs not sold in the market place, that is, provided 'free' by government.

An increase in the relative size of the non-market sector, caused for example by a transfer of workers from the market to the non-market sector, will result in greater demands for market sector goods and services by those who play no direct part in their production. The result, as shown by Johnston (1975), is excess demand for market sector outputs. This may be met by increased productivity in the market sector but the faster the relative growth of the non-market sector the higher will be the required rate of productivity growth to maintain equilibrium between supply and demand at constant prices.[1]

This can be shown by taking the identity, (3.4), derived in Chapter 3:

$$Y_m \equiv C_m + I_m + G_m + B$$

where Y_m is marketed output, C_m and I_m are purchases of marketed output by firms and workers for consumption and investment respectively, G_m is government purchases of marketed output, and B is the balance of payment current account surplus. Differentiating (3.4) with respect to time and dividing throughout by Y_m gives

$$\dot{Y}_m = a_t \dot{C}_m + \beta_t \dot{I}_m + \gamma_t \dot{G}_m + \delta_t \dot{B} \tag{9.1}$$

where a_t, β_t, γ_t and δ_t are the respective instantaneous shares of C_m, I_m, G_m and B in marketed output, Y_m, at time t, and dotted variables represent proportionate rates of change. However, if P_m is productivity or output per man in the market sector and E_m is market sector employment, then,

$$\dot{Y}_m = \dot{P}_m + \dot{E}_m \tag{9.2}$$

Combining (9.1) and (9.2) the increase in productivity required to meet the demand for marketed output at constant prices will be

$$\dot{P}_m = a_t \dot{C}_m + \beta_t \dot{I}_m + \gamma_t \dot{G}_m + \delta_t \dot{B} - \dot{E}_m \tag{9.3}$$

Now assume there is a transfer of workers from the market to the non-market sector. Further assume that this results in a fall in C_m in proportion to the decline in market sector employment, while similarly, marketed output absorbed by the non-market sector, G_m, rises in proportion to the increase in employment. Thus, the departure of any worker from the market sector does not lead to an increase in the average consumption of those workers in the market sector. This implies that the following condition must hold

$$\dot{C}_m = \dot{E}_m = -\sigma_t \dot{E}_u = -\sigma_t \dot{G}_m \tag{9.4}$$

where $\sigma_t = E_u/E_m = G_m/C_m$, at time t, and $E_u = $ non-market employment. This allows substitution of $\dot{E}_m$ and $\dot{C}_m$ in (9.3) to give (omitting time subscripts),

$$\dot{P}_m = (\gamma - \sigma(a-1))\dot{G}_m + \beta \dot{I}_m + \delta \dot{B} \tag{9.5}$$

Furthermore, if it is desired to maintain an existing equilibrium on the balance of payments, that is $\delta = 0$, $\dot{B} = O$, the required rate of growth of market sector productivity becomes

$$\dot{P}_m = (\gamma - \sigma(a-1))\dot{G}_m + \beta\dot{I}_m \qquad (9.6)$$

Clearly the required growth in productivity will increase as the process of transfer continues, that is as $a \to 0$. At the beginning of the process (when $\gamma = O$, $\sigma = O$)

$$\dot{P}_m = \beta\dot{I}_m \qquad (9.7)$$

As a tends to zero, $\dot{P}_m$ must rise to a maximum of

$$\dot{P}_m = (\sigma + \gamma)\dot{G}_m + \beta\dot{I}_m \qquad (9.8)$$

However, as $a \to O$, $\sigma \to \infty$, so that $\dot{P}_m$ similarly tends to infinity. If actual productivity growth falls short of $\dot{P}_m$, then as $\dot{E}_m \to O$, $\dot{Y}_m$ will also tend to zero.

A simple numerical example can illustrate the magnitudes involved. Assume a transfer of employment from the market to the non-market sector, no increase in market sector investment ($\dot{I}_m = O$), and that the balance of payment remains in equilibrium ($\delta\dot{B} = O$). Letting $a = 0.5$ and $\gamma = 0.4$, substitution into (9.6) gives

$$\dot{P}_m = (\gamma - \frac{\gamma}{a}(a-1))\dot{G}_m = 0.85\dot{G}_m \qquad (9.9)$$

so that for each 1 per cent rise in non-market employment, a 0.85 per cent rise in productivity in the market sector is required if all other magnitudes are to remain constant. Given zero investment growth and no overall increase in demand for marketed outputs it would be surprising if such a productivity increase was consistently achieved.

The effect of growth in the non-market sector in excess of that of marketed output must, therefore, be to reduce the share of other components of demand. Dividing the identity (3.4) by Y_m gives,

$$c_m + i_m + g_m + b_m = 1 \qquad (9.10)$$

where lower case letters stand for their respective upper case ratios. Clearly if the faster growth in G_m is not accompanied by a rise in productivity in the market sector sufficient for Y_m to grow commensurately with G_m, then g_m must rise. This in turn must affect the shares of market sector consumption and/or investment, and/or net exports. The decomposition in equation (9.10) is considered in Section 9.3 using Egyptian data for the years 1960 to 1976.

9.3 THE EGYPTIAN ECONOMY

It was shown in Chapters 7 and 8 that a problem of structural imbalance has existed in the Egyptian economy for some time. In particular, an excessive growth in employment in service sectors, especially government services, since 1960 suggests the likelihood of a rising value of g_m in equation (9.10).

Estimates of the relevant variables for the Egyptian economy between 1960 and 1976 are given in Table 9.1, with movements in the four variables shown in Figure 9.1. Before considering the data, some explanation of the calculation of the variables is necessary. In the absence of full published national accounts for Egypt, G_m has been estimated from a sectoral breakdown of public expenditure (which, in Egypt, includes many market sector activities). This includes spending on wages, direct purchases of market sector goods and services, transfers and debt service. Ideally saving out of wages should be excluded from G_m. However, unfortunately published statistics do not provide a sectoral breakdown of public expenditure between wages and non-wage payments which prevents even the application of an average savings propensity to the data.

I_m is Gross Fixed Investment by the market sector. To assess the economic implications of changes in investment it would be preferable to use net investment. However, again, separate data on capital consumption are not available. Changes in stocks have also been omitted from Table 9.1 because data are only available for years after 1965, which means that, in effect, they are absorbed into C_m which is calculated as a residual. Separate inclusion of stock changes after 1965 would, therefore, have exaggerated any downward trend in c_m from 1960 (stock changes were positive in all years but one, during 1965–76) so that it was considered preferable to use slightly inflated but consistent figures for C_m. There is, of course, an opposite effect on C_m over the whole period as a result of the inclusion in G_m of the non-consumed part of non-market sector wages.

Finally G_m, I_m and B are necessarily at market prices whereas data on Y_m can only be obtained at factor costs. It would be preferable to have all values at factor costs to avoid inaccuracies arising from changes in the average indirect tax rate. Unfortunately, this information is not available so that a further source of underestimation of C_m is created which will be increasing if the average indirect tax rate is increasing.

Doubtless, application of alternative assumptions to the data cal-

Table 9.1 The allocation of marketed output between sectors, 1960–76

	1960	1961	1962	1963	1964	1965	1966	1967	1968	1969	1970	1971	1972	1973	1974	1975	1976
Y_m (L.E. millions)	1052.7	1105.8	1156.3	1280.1	1415.9	1580.5	1684.1	1730.3	1665.1	1796.8	1979.2	2125.2	2270.3	2565.8	3084.1	3633.5	4375.4
g_m (%)	30.5	34.2	34.3	33.5	38.6	38.3	41.1	39.0	37.9	39.0	45.6	42.9	48.7	36.6	29.8	36.5	42.6
c_m (%)	57.2	50.1	53.0	58.8	45.7	47.4	42.6	46.4	51.9	49.3	45.7	50.6	44.6	55.2	68.2	57.9	40.4
i_m (%)	15.1	19.2	20.1	21.7	24.4	21.7	21.8	20.4	17.2	18.3	17.1	16.2	15.6	16.9	19.3	32.3	29.3
b_m (%)	−2.8	−3.5	−7.4	−14.0	−8.7	−7.4	−5.5	−5.8	−7.0	−6.6	−8.4	−9.7	−8.9	−8.7	−17.3	−26.7	−12.3

Notes: In the absence of a market/nonmarket classification in national account statistics Y_m has been calculated as total GDP less GDP in Social Services (SS). Included in this category are Education Health, Social and Religious Services, Security and Justice, Cultural and Recreational Services, Government Administration, and Personal Services. Some of these services are undoubtedly marketed. It is, however, difficult to know how many, and provided the share of such services in total Social Services remains fairly constant there will be little effect on any trend in Y_m. I_m is calculated as Gross Domestic Investment less Gross Domestic Investment in SS. The demands of the non-market sector on marketed output (G_m) have been estimated using data on government expenditure on non-market services from the Administration Budget current and capital accounts (1960–76). With B simply the balance of payments current account surplus, this enables i_m, g_m and hence c_m. Years up to 1971 relate to fiscal years (March to February).

Source: Gemmell (1982)

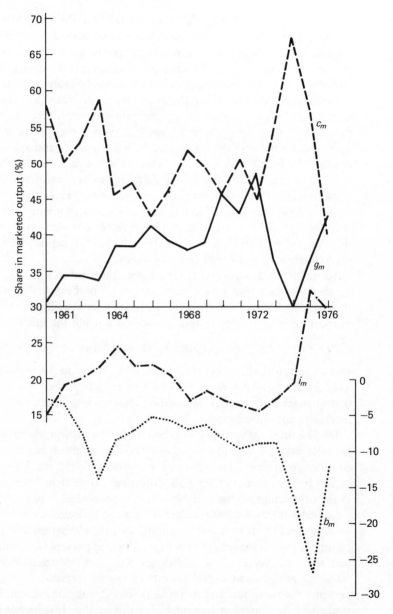

Figure 9.1   The allocation of marketed output between sectors 1960–76

Source: Gemmell (1982)

culations would yield different values for the four variables. However, the figures in Table 9.1 are not intended to establish absolute values for the sector shares but rather to show changes in the variables over the period. Calculation of c_m, for example, excluding stock change effects after 1965, does not significantly alter the overall picture in Figure 9.1.

Considering the changes in the sector shares in Figure 9.1, it can be seen firstly, that changes in g_m are primarily reflected in inverse movements in c_m. Secondly, it is clear that there is an upward trend in g_m between 1960 and 1972, followed by a sudden fall and subsequent rise to 1976. From 1965 to 1972 c_m tends to be less restricted by changes in g_m as a gradual decline in the share of market sector investment allows market sector consumption a higher share. Thus, for example, between 1966 and 1968 a decline in i_m in conjunction with a reduced value of g_m, allows a large rise in market sector consumption. Finally, the value of b_m (which is negative throughout the period) falls most sharply when c_m and i_m rise simultaneously.

To understand cause and effect between these ratios it is, of course, necessary to establish which ratio (or ratios) is the prime mover. In their study of the UK, Bacon and Eltis consider the allocation of the proportion of marketed output consumed outside the market sector $(\frac{Y_m - C_m}{Y_m} = e_m)$ between g_m, i_m and b_m. However, this does not imply that market sector workers take their share of Y_m first and the remainder is available for government, investment and exports. Indeed it is possible that changes in e_m may be affected by changes in g_m via its effects on market sector consumption.

In the context of the Egyptian economy it can be argued that g_m and to some extent i_m are the prime movers. Just as most macro models consider government expenditure as exogenous, so changes in g_m result mainly from exogenous fiscal policy decisions rather than from changes in the other endogenous variables. This is particularly apparent when increased government expenditure is financed by increases in taxation with the result that personal consumption falls. Causation in this case obviously runs from government expenditure to personal consumption and not vice versa. In a traditional Keynesian 'demand-deficient' economy government expenditure may rise in response to stagnant personal consumption and investment. But this is not relevant in the context of the Egyptian economy over this period. Investment in the market sector is to some extent subject to the same exogenous factors in Egypt as government expenditure. Much investment is carried out by public sector firms as an integral part of government development planning. Thus the rise in i_m in the early 1960s and subsequent gradual decline to 1972 reflects the movements of fiscal allocation of market sector investment funds – the intensive development effort of Egypt's First Five-Year Plan (1960–5) and the effective planlessness of the following seven years.

Figure 9.1 reveals how drastic was the effect on c_m of the rise in the share of government non-market expenditures between 1960 and 1966, c_m falling from 57 per cent in 1960 to 42 per cent in 1966. Only during 1961–3 was there any significant increase in c_m when a faster rate of growth of marketed output kept g_m fairly constant and allowed market sector consumption to expand. This took place at the expense of the balance of payments as imports rose without a compensating rise in exports. It would seem that tighter import controls after 1963 meant that when g_m continued to rise, market sector consumption and investment could no longer maintain their previous levels by absorbing imports. Thus real consumption by the market sector increased negligibly during the period and must have fallen considerably in per capita terms. It is not surprising then that government attempts to restrict consumption to provide investment funds failed, since market sector consumption was already under pressure from an unchecked growth in the non-market sector. Had this non-market expansion been restricted a larger share of domestic output could have been devoted to investment.

After a reduction in g_m and i_m between 1966 and 1968 due to the war, which enabled c_m to rise, g_m continued its upward trend to 1972. This again curtailed market sector consumption though less so than during 1960–6 because of a decline in i_m and a slight fall in b_m. Mabro and Radwan (1976) suggest that import controls were eased after 1967 and this may have helped to reduce the fall in c_m as imports increasingly supplemented domestic goods and services.

From 1972–4 a sharp fall in g_m together with a greater liberalisation of import controls in 1973, allowed a rapid rise in c_m, which was, however, reversed from 1974 when post war reconstruction and rearmament raised i_m and g_m.

Some interesting conclusions emerge from this analysis. Firstly, the growth in the claims on marketed output by the non-market sector over the 1960–76 period as a whole is undeniable, with the result that it became increasingly difficult for the market sector to supply the needs of the rest of the economy. As Table 9.2 shows, the per capita marketed output available for consumption by the market sector rose in real terms by a mere 0.2 per cent per annum. Real wages in the market

Table 9.2   The growth of real consumption in the market sector, 1960–76

	1960	1976	Average Annual Compound Rate of Change
(i) Marketed Output (at constant 1960 prices) (Y_m)	1052.7	2165.0	4.4
(ii) Market Sector Consumption (C_m)	602.1	874.7	2.4
(iii) Population dependent on the Market Sector (000s)*	21233	29728	2.0
(iv) Per Capita Market Sector Consumption [(ii) ÷ (iii)]	28.36	29.42	0.2

*Estimated as Total Population × $\dfrac{\text{Market Sector Employment}}{\text{Total Employment}}$

Source: Gemmell (1982)

sector did, of course, rise, so that effective demand was greater than available supply. This could be expected to contribute to inflation and the shortages of consumer goods which were common in Egypt over this period. What seems most likely is that those employed in the market sector who could most easily achieve wage rises maintained and even increased their consumption levels while the lower classes, with less job-security and poorer bargaining positions, suffered reductions in their consumption. The pressure on these groups obviously varied but was probably greatest during the First Five-Year Plan, when c_m fell most sharply. Indeed in 1967 an Economist Intelligence Unit report commented, 'pressure on the fixed income groups that constitute the bulk of the urban populace must be becoming intolerable'. (EIU, 1967, p. 7).

It is important to stress that this does not suggest that a rise in government spending on activities such as health or education is necessarily wrong or wasteful. These activities contribute greatly to the development effort in the long-run, but if they are allowed *in the short-run* to grow faster than the rate of growth of marketed output the result must be a reduction in the share available to other sectors. As Bacon and Eltis have pointed out, if investment and the balance of payments are not to suffer, an increase in g_m must be accompanied by a similar decline in c_m. This need not mean a reduction in the standard of living of market sector workers if that sector can achieve a satisfactory rate of output growth.[2] In Egypt, however, this has meant a negligible increase in living standards. As Figure 9.1 shows, over the period as a whole the fall in c_m largely compensated for the growth in g_m, though its failure to do so during the late 1960s and early 1970s resulted in investment in the market sector suffering and a steadily worsening balance of payments. The suggestion here is that it is the projected growth of marketed output which is crucial when deciding the allowable magnitude of non-market sector growth. Given the failure of Egyptian planners to achieve a faster rate of growth in Y_m (for whatever reasons), they could only achieve the realised increase in G_m by allowing adverse effects on other sectors. The rise in the balance of payments deficit, the squeezing of market sector investment and the restriction of many market sector workers' living standards must, therefore, be blamed partly on this expansion.

It is, however, the effects of changes in these variables on prices and output growth (via effects on employment and productivity) which are likely to be most serious for any economy and in Egypt closer examination reveals that both have been adversely affected by the increasing share of marketed output absorbed by the non-market sector.

9.4 OUTPUT, EMPLOYMENT AND PRODUCTIVITY

Normally an increase in g_m relative to c_m such as Egypt experienced between 1960 and 1976 would be expected to be accompanied by a shift in employment from the market to the non-market sector. When this occurs, as seen in Section 9.2, it raises the required rate of productivity growth if living standards are to grow equally across different sectors of workers. In Chapters 7 and 8 social service employment growth was compared with employment growth in goods-producing sectors. For present purposes, however, the relevant comparison is between growth in the market and non-market sectors.

Table 9.3 presents two estimates of market and non-market sector employment growth. The first set of estimates (1) covers the period 1960–76 and assumes the non-market sector to be equivalent to the social services sector. A second set of estimates (2) is presented for 1960–5, providing more accurate estimates of the market and non-market sectors, from a breakdown of data available only for those years. Using definition (1), non-market sector employment is estimated to be growing at about $1\frac{1}{2}$ per cent faster than that of the market sector. Comparing this with the estimate for 1960–5 using definition (2)

Table 9.3   Employment in the market and non-market sectors, 1960–76

		Employment *(in thousands)*			Average Annual Rates of Growth (%)	
		1960	*1965*	*1976*	*1960–76*	*1960–5*
Market Sector	(1)	4939.2	6067.4	7556.3	2.7	4.2
Non-Market Sector	(1)	1066.8	1306.5	2071.9	4.2	4.2
Market Sector*	(2)	5546.2	6668.4	n.a.	n.a.	3.8
Non-Market Sector†	(2)	459.8	705.5	n.a	n.a.	8.9

n.a. = not available
*Defined as employment in agriculture, industry, construction and
electricity, public utilities, housing, transport and communications, finance
and trade, personal services, and *privately-owned* health, education, social,
cultural and security services.
†Defined as employment in *publicly-owned* education, health, social, cultural
and security services, and government administration.

Source: Gemmell (1982).

suggests that definition (1) may put a downward bias on non-market
sector employment growth for the whole 1960–76 period since it clearly
does so for the first five years. However, in the absence of more
accurate data for later years this cannot be confirmed.

It was shown in Section 9.2 that, in the context of a constant total
labour force, a transfer of resources from the market to the non-market
sector will reduce the growth of marketed output unless productivity in
the market sector can rise substantially. Table 9.3 indicates that in
Egypt both market and non-market sectors have experienced increases
in employment such that a relative transfer of labour from the market
to the non-market sector has occurred. The extent to which this has
reduced $\dot{Y}_m$ can be gauged by considering the possible effects of
reducing the growth in G_m so that it increases commensurately with C_m
and comparing this with Egypt's actual experience over the period.
Results are shown in Table 9.4. On the assumption that this equalisa-
tion of $\dot{G}_m$ and $\dot{C}_m$ would likewise equalise employment growth rates
across sectors, both market and non-market employment would now
grow at 3 per cent per annum.[3] If the standard of living of market sector
workers is assumed to rise by 5 per cent over the period (that is, at 0.3
per cent per annum) instead of the actual fall of 5 per cent, this will lead
to a growth in C_m and G_m of 3.3 per cent per annum. Thus by 1976, C_m
and G_m could have risen to a total of L.E. 1552.4 million instead of L.E.
1797.0 million. Allowing the net reduction of L.E. 244.6 million in C_m

Table 9.4 Actual and projected increases in market sector supply and demands, 1960–76

(In Million Egyptian Pounds; at constant 1960 prices)			*Average Annual Rates of Growth (%) 1960–76*	
1960	*1976*			
Actual	*Actual*	*Projected*	*Actual*	*Projected*
Y_m	1052.7	2165.0	2593.9	4.6	5.8
C_m	602.1	874.7	1012.1	2.4	3.3
G_m	321.6	922.3	540.3	6.8	3.3
I_m	159.4	634.3	878.9	9.1	11.2
B	−29.8	−266.3	162.6	−14.7	12.4
		(In thousands)			
N_g	1066.8	2071.9	1706.9	4.2	3.0
N_m^g	4939.2	7556.3	7921.3	2.7	3.0
PR_m	213.1	286.5	331.5	1.9	2.8

Source: Gemmell (1982)

and G_m to be allocated to market sector investment, this might be expected to raise productivity. This relationship has been examined for Egypt using data on market sector productivity growth ($\dot{P}_m$) and investment growth ($\dot{I}_m$) for the 1960–76 period. An ordinary least squares regression produced the following result:

$$\dot{P}_m = 0.83 = 0.18\ \dot{I}_m \qquad (9.11)$$
$$\quad\ (1.28)\quad (6.88)$$

$R^2 = 0.78$; $DW = 1.53$; Figures in parenthesis are t-values. The coefficient on $\dot{I}_m$ is highly significant suggesting that a 10 per cent growth in investment could be expected to add about 2 per cent to productivity growth. Thus, as Table 9.4 shows, the result of reallocating demand is to allow market sector investment to grow at over 11 per cent per annum (instead of the previous 9 per cent), producing a productivity rise of 2.8 per cent per annum (instead of the 1.9 per cent actually achieved). Together with the 3 per cent rise in employment this would increase Y_m at an annual rate of 5.8 per cent – more than 1 per cent above the rate achieved during 1960–76.

The beneficial results of such a policy are clear. The reduced growth in the standard of living of non-market sector employees to 0.3 per cent per annum would allow a similar rise in the standard of living of the numerically much larger category of market sector employees who have actually suffered a fall in their real consumption. The balance of payments is also able to move into comfortable surplus. Alternatively some exports could be sacrificed for higher domestic consumption growth.

9.5 EFFECTS ON INFLATION

In addition to reducing output growth, the increasing demands on marketed output by those not directly concerned in its current supply will put upward pressure on prices. If productivity increases fail to maintain supply sufficient to meet demand this must be accomplished by increases in the price of marketed outputs. Johnston suggests that 'a given percentage excess demand (supply) in the current period leads to an equal percentage rise (fall) in price in the forthcoming period.' (Johnston, 1975, p. 292). Thus

$$\frac{p_{t+1}}{p_t} = a\frac{x_t}{p_t q_t} \tag{9.12}$$

where p and q are the price and quantity of marketed output respectively, x is the level of excess demand (supply) and a is a constant. Allowing for the many exogenous factors which influence p, such as rising import prices, an excess demand coefficient, a, less than unity is probably most likely, though Johnston assumes $a = 1$.

The question then arises – how is excess demand measured? There are, of course, numerous problems associated with the measurement of excess demand and particularly in a less developed economy. The unemployment rate, frequently used to measure excess demand in developed countries, is a largely meaningless statistic in most less developed countries and hence of little use for our purpose. It has been shown, however, that excess demand will arise as a result of a growth in demand by the market and non-market sectors for marketed output in excess of its supply. Thus a partial indicator of this structurally-caused excess demand will be the market sector consumption ratio c_m. As the amount of goods and services available to market sector employees is squeezed (either due to increasing government purchases, investment or exports) then, without a similar cut in wages, the result must be increased competition for available supplies, and thereby rises in prices. Prices may also be bid up indirectly as market sector employees, faced with a decline in the growth of their living standards, seek larger money wage rises which are then passed on in price increases.

Changes in the rate of growth of marketed output may also reflect changes in the pressure of demand. If in the absence of fluctuations in demand, supply grows at a constant rate, then deviations in output from this trend rate of growth may be seen as a measure of the influence of demand to raise or lower output growth. Unless supply is infinitely elastic with respect to changes in demand, a growth in demand above the trend rate of output growth will be associated with rises in prices. In fact in Egypt, as in many LDCs, there are several factors which tend to make supply inelastic. The foreign exchange shortages associated with balance of payments deficits and import controls resulted in shortages of imported input goods causing supply bottlenecks of varying degrees of severity throughout the 1960s and 1970s. Shortages of particular types of labour, despite widespread underemployment and a slow growth in agricultural productivity, similarly reduced the capacity of the economy as a whole to grow commensurately with demand. Perhaps the strongest evidence for this is the rise in the economy's balance of payments deficit. Net imports increased from -0.2 per cent of GDP in 1960 to 16.4 per cent in 1976.

The influence of these two demand variables on prices has been tested for the period 1961–76. A negative sign is to be expected on the coefficient of c_m as a falling market sector consumption ratio puts upward pressure on prices and vice versa. Conversely, a positive relationship is predicted between fluctuations in demand for marketed output and price changes. Performing an ordinary least squares regression gives the predicted signs and significant coefficients on the relevant variables. Results are shown in equation (9.13).

$$\dot{p} = 15.11 - 0.26\, c_m + 0.49\, \dot{0}^{-1} + 9.05\, D$$
$$\quad\ \ (3.69)\ \ \ (3.09)\quad\ (5.42)\quad\ \ (4.00) \tag{9.13}$$

$R^2 = 0.81$; $DW = 1.20$. Figures in parenthesis are t-values. $\dot{p}$ is the annual percentage change in wholesale prices,[4] c_m is as previously defined, and $\dot{0}^{-1}_{\ m}$ is the deviation of annual growth rates in marketed output from a constant trend rate of growth, lagged one period. D is a dummy variable for the 1973 war which created a large, exogenous influence on prices. (1973 takes a value of unity; all other years, zero.)

Both variables are significant and suggest that, on average, a 4 percentage point fall in c_m or a 2 percentage point rise in $\dot{0}^{-1}_{\ m}$ will produce a 1 percentage point rise in the rate of inflation. The important point as far as a marketed/non-marketed analysis is concerned is that if the non-market sector expands at the expense of market sector consumption it is likely to add an upward impetus to prices. Indeed in

Egypt's case it is clear that the fall in c_m, particularly during the mid-1960s and mid-1970s is partly to blame for the simultaneous surges in inflation. It is noteworthy that c_m fell by 16 percentage points 1963–6 and 28 percentage points 1974–6, while the inflation rate rose from 1.1 per cent to 7.4 per cent and 7.5 per cent to 12.4 per cent over the same periods.

9.6 COMPOSITION OF THE NON-MARKET SECTOR

These results inevitably lead to the question: could the rise in g_m have been avoided? The answer would seem to be that *in part* it could. The rates of growth of the various components of government non-market expenditure for the years when g_m increased most rapidly are shown in Table 9.5. Defence expenditure represented both the largest share and fastest growing of non-market expenditures and given the existing military situation during this time it would be unrealistic to expect any reduction in this item. However, it is also true that other areas of expenditure grew far in excess of marketed output growth. General public services grew particularly rapidly between 1960–6 (exceeding even defence expenditure increases), and 1974–6. The other main expenditure categories – education and non-market investment – also persistently exceeded marketed output growth (except 1960–6 in the case of investment). Indeed the only category which regularly grew more slowly than marketed output was local authority expenditure. It is not suggested here that these expenditures were unnecessarily high or wasteful in themselves; no doubt they involved many important and valuable projects. However, it is also the case that with the relatively low rates of marketed output growth achieved, these expenditures took place with the consequences for the rest of the economy which have already been identified. Thus a marketed/non-marketed distinction seeks only to highlight the alternatives open to planners and policy-makers. The expansion of education facilities, for example, has been a laudable goal of Egyptian planners, but the increased short-term demands which it makes on marketed output and the high levels of disguised unemployment among Egypt's educated may make a stronger case for channelling some of that expenditure into sectors which raise current supplies of marketed output. Similarly, the growth in expenditure on government services which allows high graduate underemployment in public administration could almost certainly benefit the economy more if it was used in the market sector.

Table 9.5 Growth of non-market expenditures, 1960–76

	Share of total Expenditure in 1960	(at constant 1960 prices) Average Annual Rates of Growth (%)			
		1960–76	1960–6	1968–72	1974–6
Current Expenditures					
General Public Services	21.8	5.0	19.2	0.9	22.0
Defence	23.7	7.0	17.5	5.7	13.4
Including Emergency Fund	—	10.5	—	22.0	38.7
Education	13.9	6.4	9.4	6.9	12.8
Health	2.7	10.1	15.0	15.4	–8.3
Community & Social	1.0	10.1	22.3	–15.9	150.0
Local Government	11.2	2.6	–2.0	0.7	24.3
Investment Expenditures	18.7	6.8	–2.6	13.0	77.0
Total	100	6.8	10.6	12.8	32.0
Marketed Output	—	4.6	5.1	5.8	9.0

Source: Gemmell (1982)

9.7 SUMMARY AND CONCLUSIONS

This chapter has attempted to show some of the consequences of changes in the composition of demand for market sector goods and services. In Section 9.2 it was shown that increases in the relative size of the non-market sector raise the required rate of productivity growth if marketed output is not to be retarded and inflationary pressures avoided. Section 9.3 investigated the effects of growing public expenditure on non-marketed outputs in the Egyptian economy since 1960 and it was suggested that this was at least partly to blame for a worsening balance of payments, reductions in market sector consumption and insufficient market sector investment over the period. Furthermore, it was shown in Sections 9.4 and 9.5 that this expansion of the non-market sector has reduced output growth and added to inflationary pressures. Disaggregating non-market expenditures in Section 9.6 indicated that increasing defence expenditure, the item usually blamed for the rising government budget deficit, did indeed contribute substantially to the relative growth of the non-market sector. However, most other expenditures grew in excess of marketed output, of which the most significant were education and government administration expenditures.

The effects of non-market sector growth considerred in this chapter are short-run; no predictions are made for the long-run. The history of growth in many developed countries is of a rising contribution of such non-marketed outputs as education and health facilities, and many would argue that they are an important source of rises in productivity throughout an economy. If, however, the non-market sector grows rapidly in the short-term its demands on marketed outputs are likely to exceed greatly its contribution to their supply. This has been the case in Egypt, at least during 1960–76. If the resulting problems are to be avoided in the future, Egyptian planners must initially attempt to equalise the rates of growth of G_m and Y_m until a sufficiently high rate of growth of marketed output can be achieved to allow an increasing share to be purchased by the non-market sector without this putting excessive pressure on other sectors. If instead present trends are allowed to continue the outcome must be slower growth than would otherwise occur, increasing foreign indebtedness, greater social unrest and further inflationary pressures.

Part IV
Results and Prospects

10 Summary and Conclusions

10.1 INTRODUCTION

This book has been concerned primarily with three related aspects of the growth of service sectors during development. It was desired firstly to examine the extent of uniformity across countries in patterns of structural change involving service sectors. Secondly, since the growth of publicly-owned, non-marketed services has been prominent in many countries this study has attempted to examine and compare some of the likely effects of such an expansion. The growth in non-marketed services has caused problems of government finance in several countries in recent years, as tax revenues have proved less easy to raise than government expenditure. This book has therefore examined the built-in flexibility properties of various widely used taxes in developed countries in order to assess the prospects for tax revenue growth. Finally, following a review of service sector case studies in a number of less developed countries, a case study of the Egyptian economy from 1960 to the mid-1970s was undertaken. This examined the aspects of service growth during development discussed above, and sought to explain the rapid growth in service sector employment observed in Egypt over this period.

The results and conclusions of this study will be summarised in this chapter in three sections. Section 10.2 summarises the evidence on structural change towards services identified internationally (in Chapter 2) and from case studies of less developed countries (in Chapters 6–8). Possible reasons for this phenomenon in less developed countries, suggested by the case study evidence, are also assessed in Section 10.2. Section 10.3 then examines the role of a market/non-market distinction in analysing countries' overall macroeconomic performance, and particularly that of Egypt. In Section 10.4 the results of the tax models considered in Chapters 4 and 5 are summarised and some conclusions drawn.

179

10.2 STRUCTURAL CHANGE TOWARDS SERVICES

10.2.1 Cross-section evidence

Chapter 2 examined the hypotheses that there were uniform patterns of structural change across developed and less developed countries. Previous studies had suggested that while industrial and agricultural sector shares of employment tend to rise and fall respectively in similar patterns across countries as per capita income increases, this is less true for service sectors. Recent evidence has also identified a decline in industrial sectors in many developed countries accompanied by a rise in services, including government services. If this phenomenon is widely experienced among developed countries it implies that the forms of equations previously used to test for cross-section patterns of structural change involving services may mistakenly fail to identify common patterns across countries. Chapter 2 proposed alternative functional forms which could capture the effects of 'de-industrialisation' in developed countries. If the pattern of service and industrial employment shares rising together in the early stages of development but the service share increasing *at the expense of* the industrial share in later stages of development is a general one, the proposed functional forms could be expected to provide a good fit to the data.

Evidence from an international sample for 1960 and 1970 provided strong support for the view that uniform patterns of the sort described above exist for the sectoral employment shares. Two caveats to this general conclusion, however, seemed warranted. Firstly, the tests indicated that there was more divergence from the predicted patterns in 1970 than in 1960, from which it would appear that factors affecting employment shares which are specific to particular countries were more prominent in 1970 than 1960. Although the divergence appears to occur for both developed and developing countries the reasons are probably different for each group. These reasons were not investigated in this book though two possibilities suggest themselves.

Firstly, among developing countries *some* have experienced considerable increases in 'informal' urban services (mainly those countries with high population growth and migration rates) while others have not. Substantial increases in 'informal' activities in those countries began during the 1960s and this may partly account for the divergence among developing countries.

Secondly, for developed countries the phenomenon of de-industrialisation was not as widespread by 1970 as it has subsequently become. Thus the 1970 evidence may represent a 'snapshot' of a transition period in which some countries' industrial sectors are still expanding while others have already begun to decline. In cross-section evidence a temporary divergence between developed countries in their patterns of structural change would therefore be observed.

A second caveat to the general conclusion of uniform cross-country patterns concerns the particularly large values of, and increase in, the service employment share in some Latin American countries, mainly Brazil, Peru, Mexico and Argentina. The evidence of large increases in the social service employment shares in Chapters 2 and 6 points to the possibility that in these 'middle-income' countries early expansion of government services has occurred. This seems to be partly in response to an excess supply of *educated* manpower created by government policies, which those governments then employ.

The results in Chapter 2 suggest some further properties to the cross-country patterns. Firstly service employment appears to expand relative to industry in the early and late stages of development with industrial employment expanding most in the 'middle' phase. Within the service sector, social services follow a similar pattern – expanding relative to other services in the early and late stages of development. It seems likely that this important 'early' role for social services, while it is true for LDCs today, was probably less true for the developed countries in the early stages of their development. It is often the post-colonial legacy of large government bureaucracies and government objectives of universal education for their populations in many LDCs today which accounts for their relatively large share of employment in social services. These factors were not generally present in developed countries' early development.

Finally the approach in Chapter 2 was mainly concerned with cross-section patterns and although some evidence of changes within countries over time was considered, time-series patterns were not rigorously investigated. The limited time-series evidence that was examined was generally consistent with the cross-section result but it must be stressed that predictions of structural changes over time, based on cross-country results must be made with caution. The evidence considered in Chapter 2 is consistent with previous studies in suggesting that while broad indications of *long-run* changes through time may be obtained from cross-section evidence, these international patterns do shift over time. Until longer-term time-series data are available for LDCs it would, therefore, be unwise to predict that as they develop they will necessarily follow the cross-section patterns observed. Indeed the growth of some services (such as 'informal' services) are specific to LDCs and it is still unclear how their share of employment will change as per capita incomes rise.

10.2.2 Case study evidence

Evidence on service sector growth from previous studies of a number of less developed countries was presented in Chapter 6, and it is clear that some of these countries have unusually large service sectors even by the standards of developed countries (e.g. Israel, Singapore). However, the evidence also suggested that the phenomenon of relatively large service sectors is more widespread among less developed countries than might have been thought. Within services, a number of studies highlighted a particularly dominant role for trade services (mainly retail) and publicly-provided 'other services' – administration, health, education, etc.

Evidence from Egypt in Chapter 7 indicated that the service sector's employment share during 1960–75 was substantially above that predicted from an international sample, and had been since at least the 1930s. A relative growth in services was occurring both in commercial and in social services, of which government administration and education displayed especially rapid growth. Although defence services are excluded from Egyptian employment data, government espenditure data, examined in Chapter 9, suggested that these services also expanded rapidly over the period, as would be expected given the military situation at the time.

Chapter 8 examined the role of income elasticity differences, wage rate differences and productivity growth differences between sectors as explanations of relative service employment growth in Egypt. Data and methodological limitations permit only tentative conclusions, but it did seem that income elasticity differences between sectors were unlikely to explain the observed employment differences. There was some evidence (though it could not be considered strong) that employment in different sectors did respond to changes in wage rates, but differential responses across sectors could not be confirmed.

Evidence in Chapter 8 also suggested that inter-sectoral differences in productivity growth were highly variable both across service subsectors and across different time periods, and there was certainly no general evidence of slower productivity growth in services. Examining sectoral differences in productivity growth did, however, provide clues to some of the influences on relative service employment growth. Two factors were identified in particular. Firstly, government education and employment policies have resulted in distortions in the skill composition of the labour force with an excess supply of educated manpower, especially university graduates from Arts faculties. To prevent unemployment the government regularly absorbed this surplus into its public service sector.

Secondly, high rates of population growth and rural to urban migration swelled the number of urban job seekers during the 1960s and 1970s. At the same time indecision in the implementation of Egypt's five-year plans and a lack of direction in the publicly-owned manufacturing sector caused the demand for labour to grow particularly slowly in a large part of the goods-producing sector after 1965. Much of the surplus urban labour therefore found its way into privately-owned informal services.

The evidence from Egypt and the other less developed countries considered in Part 3, suggests a number of similarities across countries in the factors influencing service sector growth, as well as some which are specific to particular economies. Firstly, *general* evidence of higher income elasticities for, or slower productivity growth in, services in less developed countries has not found support. Nevertheless, demand has clearly been an important influence on the growth of some services. It appears that for some informal services (e.g. transport, retailing, personal services) demands have increased both because of the growth of urban 'squatter' communities who cannot afford 'modern' transport or retailing services, and because of improvements in the standard of living for higher income earners, who use informal laundering, child-minding services, etc.

The growth of these poor urban communities appears also to have created demands for more formal services such as transport and public utilities. Many less developed countries have found their urban roads, drainage, sewage and power services under increasing pressure in recent years, due to urban congestion. This has created, and is likely to create, further pressures to expand and improve existing services.

The prominence of public services in overall service expansion in a number of the countries examined points to the importance of government policy as a determinant of the relative growth of services. Evidence on Egypt, Israel and a number of Latin American countries highlighted how governments may expand services by interfering with the market mechanism. The situation in Egypt, where the government fixes wages in many areas of the economy and independently determines the level of education provision does not seem uncommon. The result, not surprisingly, is often an excess supply of educated manpower, which governments then employ, especially in public services. In Israel it was noted that government policy on education and health provision had strongly influenced the expansion of these services. Indeed, in a number of less developed countries governments have borrowed heavily to enable substantial expansion in these services. This serves to make the market/non-market taxonomy particularly relevant to those countries.

Finally, many studies have attributed an important role to rural-urban migration (or international migration in Israel's case) in explaining informal service growth, though there are numerous problems reliably identifying causality here. Nevertheless, it is clear that in many less developed countries migration rates are persistently exceeding growth rates of 'modern' employment opportunities, and informal services grow, to some extent, as a 'residual'. As is now known, this need not mean that the informal sector is unproductive and purely supply-determined. It is interesting to note that, although the informal sector is associated almost exclusively with less developed countries today, it may well have played a similar role in at least some developed countries' earlier industrial development. Frederick Engels, for example, identified a 'reserve army' of unemployed labour in nineteenth century England, who were 'surplus' to the labour demands of manufacturing industry. He argues that 'this reserve army ... is the "surplus population" of England, which keeps body and soul together by begging, stealing, street-sweeping, collecting manure, pushing handcarts, driving donkeys, peddling or performing occasional small jobs. In every great town a multitude of such people are to be found. It is astonishing in what devices this "surplus population" takes refuge' (Engels, 1892, p. 85). Such statements could be made with reference to the informal sectors of any of a number of today's developing countries.

10.3 NON-MARKET SECTOR GROWTH

Building on the work of Johnston (1975) and Bacon and Eltis (1976) Chapter 3 suggested a framework in which differences in the rates of growth of market and non-market sector employment could be compared across countries. In particular it was desired to examine the extent to which different countries' macroeconomic performance varied with expansion of the non-market sector. The macroeconomic variables considered were per capita consumption growth, investment growth and the balance of payments.

It was shown in Chapter 3 that, *ex post*, the faster the rate of total employment growth relative to marketed output growth the slower must be combined growth in per capita consumption, investment and the balance of payments surplus. Two particular effects of growth in non-market sector employment may, however, be identified. Firstly, while growth in employment in the market sector may be expected, via the production function relationship, to raise marketed output, growth in non-market sector employment creates demand for marketed outputs, but does not directly contribute to their current supply. Multiplier effects may indeed encourage faster marketed output growth but, as Johnston has argued, it is likely that some short-run excess demand for marketed output will be created, requiring market sector productivity to rise, or causing inflation.

Secondly, Bacon and Eltis have argued that if non-market sector growth is financed by taxation, unless tax payers are willing to accept reductions in disposable income, the effect may be to generate inflationary pressures. If wage earners are taxed and succeed in raising money wages to maintain real consumption, investment and the balance of payments can be expected to suffer.

It was, therefore, of particular interest to examine in Chapter 3 *non-market* employment growth relative to marketed output growth which might be expected to affect macroeconomic performance particularly adversely. Empirical evidence from a sample of developed and less developed countries (considering growth rates over the period 1960–1970) suggested that many LDCs in particular experienced high rates of growth of marketed output, total and non-market employment. It did not seem to be the case, however, that either developed or less developed countries as a group experienced greater constraints in aggregate on the macroeconomic variables considered. This constraint appeared to be greatest for the United States, the UK and Egypt, all countries in which previous studies had suggested non-market growth may have had serious adverse effects. It was also found that for a given rate of market sector productivity growth, employment in non-market sectors was expanding especially rapidly (relative to marketed output) in LDCs. This confirms the suggestion in Chapter 2 that the rapid expansion of social service employment in many LDCs has occurred prior to, or without, commensurate increases in marketed output.

Chapter 9 examined the role of non-market sector growth in Egypt

during 1960–75. It was shown that the share of marketed output going
to the non-market sector, g_m, rose considerably over the period.
Movements in this share were generally mirrored by inverse movements
in the proportion of marketed output available for consumption by
those in the market sector, c_m. It was also argued that in Egypt market
sector productivity growth was a positive function of investment in that
sector and that a reallocation of resources from government consumption to market sector investment could have had significant effects on
marketed output growth.

It was noted above that non-market sector expansion could be
expected to increase inflationary pressures, especially if this reduced
market sector workers' share of marketed output. The hypothesis that
reductions in the proportion of marketed output consumed by the
market sector, c_m, would increase inflation was therefore tested, and
found to significantly affect the inflation rate.

In examining the relationship between market and non-market
sectors it has been stressed that the methodology adopted does not
investigate causal relationships between variables. The 'Bacon and Eltis
identity' (given in equation 9.11) expresses only the *ex post* relationship
between the sector shares in marketed output and observed changes in
these shares may be the outcome of a number of complex, inter-related
changes in the various variables. Chrystal (1983) has summed up the
approach as follows:

> The Bacon and Eltis taxonomy undoubtedly provides an interesting
> framework within which to view the economy. However, their
> methodology at best establishes correlations but not causation. (p.
> 139).

While this may be accepted, it should not prevent consideration of the
likely causal mechanisms inherent in the observed correlations. It must,
therefore, be on the basis of *a priori* reasoning that the direction of
causality between variables in the identity may be established. Thus, for
example, it has been argued that a 'crowding out' effect of an increase
in g_m is more likely when the economy is fully employed than when
unemployed resources exist. In Egypt's case it was argued that government control of a large proportion of production and the planning
policy it has followed make it more plausible that an increasing share of
marketed output consumed and invested by government has in part
caused the reduction in resources available to other sectors. However, it
is clear that more theoretical and empirical work on the relationships

between market and non-market sectors is necessary in order to clarify some of the issues of causation. It may also be noted that not only does the extent of the resource shift from market to non-market sectors vary across countries, (as evidenced in Chapter 3) but the causal mechanisms may similarly vary. It is important, therefore, that conclusions on the nature of market/non-market sector relationships in particular countries are based on individual country studies.

Finally the results obtained in Chapter 3 indicate that high rates of growth of non-market sector employment (relative to market sector output and employment growth) are common to many countries. The required increase in government expenditure to enable this growth must be financed by taxation and/or government borrowing. The ability to finance these expenditure increases is important for their continued growth and this study has therefore examined the prospects for tax revenue growth. These are summarised below.

10.4 TAX REVENUE GROWTH

In order to examine how tax revenues can be expected to change as per capita income rises, Chapter 4 investigated the built-in flexibility properties of a progressive income tax using a model which could approximate many actual systems in use. In Chapter 5 this was integrated into a wider fiscal model which enabled examination of the built-in flexibility properties of a number of inter-related taxes. In both chapters elements of the UK tax system were approximated. However, since several developed countries operate broadly similar systems (which vary primarily in the way taxes are levied and in the nature of the interdependencies between taxes) it was argued that the model could be adapted to examine other tax systems.

In Chapter 4 a non-linear income tax structure was used in conjunction with a lognormal distribution of income, to obtain schedules for effective average and marginal tax rates and elasticities, as per capita income increases. As may be expected effective average and marginal rates were found to rise with income increases. However, the effective average rate schedule was sigmoid in shape, rising steeply at relatively low average income levels, but becoming fairly 'flat' at high average incomes. The revenue elasticity which declined as average income increased, also appeared to become almost constant at higher average incomes.

Examining the built-in flexibility of the tax/transfer model in

Chapter 5, it was clear that this was a function of different forms of tax threshold indexation and the rates of inflation and real earnings growth. Effective average tax rate (EAR) results were presented for an inflation rate of 5 per cent and real earnings growth of 2 per cent. The results suggested that although the built-in flexibility of all taxes was removed in the extreme case of all tax/transfer thresholds indexed to nominal earnings, in the more likely cases of some threshold indexation equal to or less than the rate of price increases, significant flexibility remained. Effective average rates of income tax for example rose significantly as average income increased, especially when compared with other tax revenue schedules. National Insurance EAR schedules displayed little (though slightly downward) built-in flexibility as may be expected from their slight regressivity.

VAT revenue possesses little flexibility due to its structure, but effective average rates were found to fall slightly in most cases, due to the effects of income tax and transfers on the VAT tax base – expenditure. The effective average transfer was also observed to decrease as average income increased, in most cases. Indeed it seemed likely that unless transfer payments were linked to nominal earnings they would be expected to become less generous. In the UK system where some individuals both pay tax and receive benefits, transfers were found to be sensitive to income tax indexation.

These results allow some general observations on changes in tax revenues resulting from income growth. Firstly, it would seem that at higher average income levels (that is, those relevant to developed countries) the capacity of the tax system to generate automatic increases in tax revenue is particularly limited. The growth of net revenue, which is mainly affected by income tax revenue growth, was shown to be increasing relative to average income but at a diminishing rate, as average income rises. At higher average income levels the profiles are fairly 'flat' compared to lower income levels. This is of particular concern from the point of view of funding government expenditure increases, since evidence in Chapter 2 suggested that a relative growth in publicly-provided services is particularly rapid in developed countries. If automatic revenue increases are less, then for a given increase in expenditure relative to average income, greater reliance on tax rate changes or other adjustments to the tax structure is required, or greater use of borrowing. This last alternative may, of course, simply widen the gap between expenditure and required tax revenue at higher average income levels (if incomes grow over time).

Secondly, National Insurance and VAT cannot be relied upon to produce significant revenue increases as average income increases. Indeed it would seem that the slight regressivity of NI is most likely to reduce effective average rates of NI, while VAT revenue is also likely to decrease (relative to average income) due to the progressivity of income tax. However, compared to income tax, effective average rates of NI and VAT change very little under plausible indexation assumptions, as average income increases. In addition, to obtain any increase in EARs of VAT it was found to be necessary to index income tax thresholds such that income tax EAR schedules became horizontal.

Thirdly, income growth, as may be expected, is in general associated with a declining share of resources devoted to transfer payments as fewer individuals remain eligible. However, the form of indexation of benefits is important for changes in the 'effective average transfer', $T/\bar{y}$. Indexation at the rate of growth of earnings will, if real earnings growth is positive, cause $T/\bar{y}$ to rise as average income rises, so increasing the burden of financing transfer payments. Keeping real benefits constant, however, does allow the financing burden to decline with income growth.

In the UK the National Insurance scheme is not 'self-financing', that is, total contributions are not expected to cover the total cost of transfers (unemployment benefit, pensions, etc.) paid from the fund, nor are contribution rates necessarily changed in line with changes in payments. Nevertheless, the results in Chapter 5 indicate that financing certain transfers from National Insurrance could become more difficult as incomes grow since earnings indexation of benefits raises $T/\bar{y}$, while price indexation of NI thresholds reduces $R_c/\bar{y}$. This combination of indexations could certainly occur in practice although in the UK recently benefit levels have not typically increased in line with nominal earnings.

Finally, this book has not been concerned primarily with the *causes* of structural changes. Rather it has examined patterns of structural change, some implications of non-market sector growth, and profiles or 'patterns' of tax revenue growth. In the Egyptian case study it was desired to establish factors causing service sector employment growth but since Egypt was shown to be a fairly extreme example of this phenomenon, it could not be presumed to indicate causal factors elsewhere. In addition, a number of causal mechanisms identified in some less developed countries in Chapter 6 appeared to be country-specific. It does seem, moreover, that in seeking to understand the processes of structural change involving private and public service sector growth, the causal mechanisms at work are the most difficult to identify, and verify. Unfortunately, economic theory and empirical evidence have frequently been unable to offer unambiguous guidance, yet it is undoubtedly in this area that progress needs to be made. Hopefully, future research will be able to shed more light on these difficult issues.

Appendices

Appendices

APPENDIX 1 REVENUE, ELASTICITY AND EFFECTIVE MARGINAL RATE SCHEDULES (Without a Standard Rate)

Schedules presented in Chapter 4 were obtained from the non-linear income tax function which included a 'standard' tax rate over a fairly wide range of incomes. However, a number of countries have progressive personal income taxes which do not include a standard rate (e.g. West Germany, USA). Figure A1.1 presents revenue schedules comparable to those in Figure 4.2 but without a standard rate, and similar elasticity and EMR schedules are given in Figure A1.2.

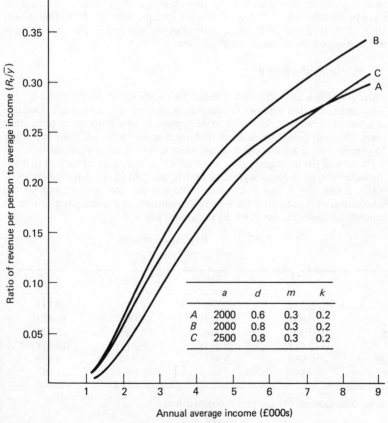

	a	d	m	k
A	2000	0.6	0.3	0.2
B	2000	0.8	0.3	0.2
C	2500	0.8	0.3	0.2

Figure A1.1   Total income tax revenue

Comparing Figures 4.2 and A1.1 it can be seen that in the absence of a standard rate of income tax the revenue schedules no longer display the approximately linear section between about £5000 and £9000. The overall sigmoid shape evident in the standard rate case is therefore enhanced in the non-standard-rate case. Some interesting differences also occur in the elasticity and EMR schedules (Figures 4.3 and A1.2). Elasticities, which became almost constant between £5000 and £9000 before continuing to decrease, in the standard rate case, now show a fairly uniform decline in Figure A1.2. Conversely, EMRs can be seen to increase at a diminishing rate between £5000 and £9000 in Figure A1.2, whereas in Figure 4.3 they were increasing almost uniformly.

APPENDIX 2 THE VAT SCHEDULE

To test for changes in the relationships between expenditure, q, and the proportion of expenditure on zero-rated goods, $r(q)$, as incomes changed over time, regressions on equation (5.4) were examined. FES (weekly) data for all households together, covering 16 income groups, were used for four years; 1973, 1975, 1979 and 1980. These years allow shorter and longer term changes to be observed. Regressions took the form

$$log \ r(q) = \alpha^* - \beta log \ q$$

where $\alpha^* = \log \alpha$ in (5.4). These yielded the results shown in Table A2.1.

It can be seen that while α^* increases through time, β remains approximately constant at about 0.34. The 1979 value appears to be slightly lower than other years. This may be due to effects of the large increase in the VAT rate in 1979 to 15 percent, but if so, this effect would seem to have been temporary.

Examining the increase in α^* it was found that this changed such as to leave the value of $r(q)$ at mean expenditure fairly constant at about 0.45. (Values of 0.451, 0.453, 0.487 and 0.451 were obtained for the four years.) In the simulations in the tax model α is therefore adjusted to maintain $r(q)$, at mean expenditure, constant (as given by equation (5.5).

Table A2.1 Regression results

	1973	1975	1979	1980
α^*	0.478	0.593	0.654	0.785
	(0.043)	(0.049)	(0.063)	(0.083)
β	−0.347	−0.346	−0.302	−0.336
	(0.012)	(0.013)	(0.014)	(0.018)
R^2	0.985	0.981	0.970	0.961
n	14	16	16	16

Note: Standard errors are given in parentheses

Source: Creedy and Gemmell (1985)

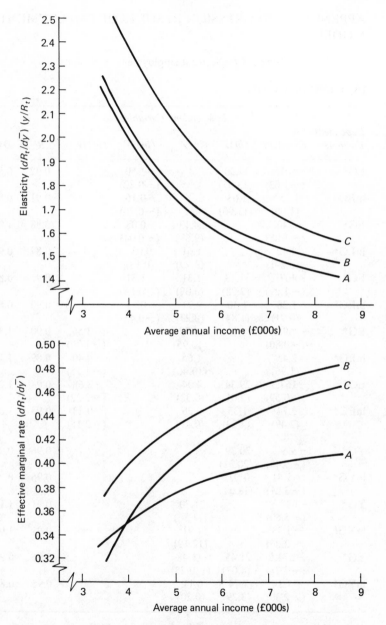

Figure A1.2   Elasticities and effective marginal rates (without standard rate)

APPENDIX 3   REGRESSION RESULTS OF EMPLOYMENT MODEL

Table A3.1   Sectoral employment regressions

(A) Goods* Sector (G*)

Dependent Variable	Constant	$(ln)Z$	$(ln)Z_{-1}$	$(ln)W_i$	$(ln)W_{i,-1}$	R^2	DW
			Independent Variables				
EG*	−501.1	33.30		−1.50		0.92	0.86
	(−1.62)	(13.07)		(−0.82)			
lnEG*	1.25	1.63		−0.16		0.91	0.82
	(1.00)	(11.90)		(−0.70)			
EG*	−740.3		34.13	−0.08		0.88	1.05
	(−1.88)		(9.68)	(−0.04)			
lnEG*	0.42		1.61	0.03		0.87	0.94
	(0.29)		(9.29)	(0.13)			
EG*	−467.2	31.13	1.31	−1.31		0.92	0.85
	(−1.29)	(2.28)	(0.09)	(−0.66)			
lnEG*	1.28	1.36	0.21	−0.11		0.90	0.81
	(0.91)	(1.84)	(0.27)	(−0.45)			
EG*	−269.2		35.72		−3.56	0.90	1.32
	(−0.80)		(10.95)		(−1.79)		
lnEG*	2.45		1.65		−0.40	0.89	1.15
	(1.96)		(10.46)		(−1.75)		
EG*	−167.3	29.34	4.04		−3.68	0.94	1.22
	(−0.59)	(2.61)	(0.32)		(−2.22)		
lnEG*	2.74	1.35	0.26		−0.43	0.93	1.07
	(2.49)	(2.23)	(0.41)		(−2.15)		
YG*	−599.8	20.39				0.96	0.92
	(−9.40)	(20.31)					
lnYG*	−1.41	1.91				0.96	0.74
	(−3.21)	(18.01)					
YG*	−637.3		21.70			0.91	1.14
	(−5.60)		(11.86)				
lnYG*	−1.33		1.91			0.91	1.09
	(−2.06)		(12.19)				
YG*	−574.5	21.45	−1.48			0.96	0.98
	(−7.21)	(4.07)	(−0.25)				
lnYG*	−1.14	1.74	0.11			0.95	0.83
	(−2.30)	(3.29)	(0.20)				

Notes: All regressions shown are either linear or double-log forms, as indicated by the form of the dependent variable. Results from semi-log regressions were in general slightly poorer than those of linear or log-log regressions and are not presented. The aggregate goods sector functions were also tested but did not perform well. This may be expected because trends in agricultural employment are obviously very different from trends in non-agricultural goods employment. Factors affecting agricultural employment are also likely to be different.

EG* = employment in the goods* sector
YG* = output from the goods* sector
Z = per capita GDP
W_i = average annual wage in sector i
DW = Durbin-Watson statistic

Figures in parentheses are t-statistics

Table A3.1   continued   (B) **Total services (S)**

Dependent Variable	Constant	$(ln)Z$	$(ln)Z_{-1}$	$(ln)W_i$	$(ln)W_{i,-1}$	R^2	DW
			Independent Variables				
ES	651.7	52.28		−7.28		0.96	1.02
	(1.50)	(19.18)		(−2.90)			
lnES	5.52	1.30		−0.58		0.96	1.03
	(5.94)	(18.00)		(−3.04)			
ES	79.46		55.89	−4.76		0.96	1.56
	(0.16)		(17.66)	(−1.81)			
lnES	4.42		1.32	−0.38		0.96	1.47
	(4.55)		(17.30)	(−2.01)			
ES	485.1	27.86	26.16	−6.64		0.97	1.10
	(1.06)	(2.32)	(1.99)	(−2.76)			
lnES	5.18	0.64	0.67	−0.52		0.97	1.10
	(5.40)	(1.97)	(1.99)	(−2.81)			
ES	160.9		58.02		−5.93	0.97	1.95
	(0.39)		(18.25)		(−2.40)		
lnES	4.53		1.37		−0.44	0.96	1.91
	(5.30)		(17.47)		(−2.44)		
ES	240.5	18.05	38.61		−6.11	0.97	1.62
	(0.61)	(1.56)	(3.02)		(−2.60)		
lnES	4.67	0.37	1.00		−0.46	0.97	1.67
	(5.50)	(1.19)	(3.06)		(−2.59)		
YS	−1066.1	30.49				0.98	0.86
	(−14.35)	(26.08)					
lnYS	−2.50	2.23				0.98	1.01
	(−7.76)	(28.53)					
YS	−1215.8		33.89			0.96	1.52
	(−10.51)		(18.20)				
lnYS	−2.91		2.34			0.97	1.81
	(−6.56)		(21.72)				
YS	−1152.7	21.57	10.59			0.98	0.86
	(−13.99)	(3.96)	(1.76)				
lnYS	−2.77	1.30	1.00			0.99	1.08
	(−8.80)	(3.90)	(2.89)				

Notes: ES = employment in the service sector
         YS = output from the service sector

Table A3.1   continued

(C) **Commercial services** (CS)

Dependent Variable	Constant	$(\ln)Z$	$(\ln)Z_{-1}$	$(\ln)W_i$	$(\ln)W_{i,-1}$	R^2	DW
			Independent Variables				
ECS	333.1	17.82		−2.47		0.97	1.21
	(2.51)	(21.11)		(−2.61)			
lnECS	4.34	1.03		−0.32		0.97	1.20
	(7.08)	(20.26)		(−2.58)			
ECS	96.76		18.99	−0.996		0.96	1.62
	(0.57)		(17.27)	(−0.91)			
lnECS	3.46		1.04	−0.148		0.96	1.56
	(4.85)		(17.71)	(−1.11)			
ECS	328.17	12.14	5.80	−2.37		0.98	1.55
	(2.09)	(2.91)	(1.26)	(−2.40)			
lnECS	4.31	0.63	0.39	−0.30		0.97	1.54
	(6.32)	(2.57)	(1.48)	(−2.40)			
ECS	279.9		19.30		−2.47	0.97	1.34
	(2.27)		(21.86)		(−2.94)		
lnECS	4.18		1.06		−0.31	0.98	1.30
	(8.06)		(22.49)		(−3.05)		
ECS	299.8	7.29	11.43		−2.46	0.98	0.80
	(2.79)	(2.28)	(3.23)		(−3.36)		
lnECS	4.24	0.36	0.69		−0.31	0.98	0.85
	(8.98)	(1.94)	(3.46)		(−3.40)		
YCS	−254.6	9.49				0.91	0.88
	(−5.35)	(12.66)					
lnYCS	−1.07	1.66				0.91	0.96
	(−1.98)	(12.68)					
YCS	−289.2		10.36			0.87	1.13
	(−4.36)		(9.70)				
lnYCS	−1.20		1.71			0.87	1.08
	(−1.65)		(9.65)				
YCS	−264.1	8.58	1.09			0.90	0.87
	(−4.38)	(2.15)	(0.25)				
lnYCS	−1.05	1.41	0.25			0.90	0.92
	(−1.58)	(1.99)	(0.34)				

Notes: ECS = employment in the commercial services sector
YCS = output from the commercial services sector

Table A3.1   continued

(D) **Social services** (SS)

Dependent Variable	Constant	$(ln)Z$	$(ln)Z_{-1}$	$(ln)W_i$	$(ln)W_{i,-1}$	R^2	DW
				Independent Variables			
ESS	120.64	33.33		−3.33		0.95	0.87
	(0.42)	(16.75)		(−2.48)			
lnESS	4.34	1.44		−0.56		0.94	0.88
	(3.82)	(15.06)		(−2.55)			
ESS	−171.1		36.33	−2.51		0.95	1.34
	(−0.57)		(16.53)	(−1.94)			
lnESS	3.36		1.49	−0.41		0.95	1.27
	(3.03)		(15.22)	(−2.02)			
ESS	−38.77	13.96	21.32	−2.95		0.96	0.90
	(−0.13)	(1.57)	(2.17)	(−2.35)			
lnESS	3.76	0.50	0.98	−0.47		0.95	0.96
	(3.26)	(1.14)	(2.11)	(−2.28)			
ESS	−329.1		37.14		−2.01	0.95	1.77
	(−1.14)		(15.05)		(−1.42)		
lnESS	2.70		1.53		−0.31	0.94	1.69
	(2.41)		(13.57)		(−1.38)		
ESS	−279.4	10.29	26.09		−2.12	0.95	1.50
	(−0.96)	(1.07)	(2.45)		(−1.50)		
lnESS	2.82	0.31	1.22		−0.33	0.94	1.54
	(2.43)	(0.65)	(2.45)		(−1.42)		
YSS	−811.4	20.99				0.96	0.74
	(−11.85)	(19.49)					
lnYSS	−4.72	2.63				0.95	0.63
	(−7.58)	(17.49)					
YSS	−926.6		23.53			0.95	1.21
	(−10.42)		(16.45)				
lnYSS	−5.35		2.81			0.95	1.15
	(−7.56)		(16.34)				
YSS	−888.6	12.99	9.49			0.97	0.72
	(−11.59)	(2.56)	(1.69)				
lnYSS	−5.21	1.20	1.56			0.96	0.69
	(−7.81)	(1.70)	(2.08)				

Notes: ESS = employment in social services
YSS = output from social services

Table A3.2   Sectoral employment change regressions

Dependent Variable	Constant	$\Delta(ln)Z$	$\Delta(ln)Z_{-1}$	$\Delta(ln)W_i$	$\Delta(ln)W_{i,-1}$	R^2	DW
			Independent Variables				
ΔEG^*	0.92 (1.99)	−0.06 (−0.12)		0.19 (1.25)		0.11	1.88
$\Delta lnEG^*$	0.91 (3.46)	−0.04 (−0.15)		0.14 (1.30)		0.12	1.84
ΔEG^*	1.76 (3.82)		−0.66 (−1.42)		−0.03 (−0.18)	0.16	0.79
ΔES	1.00 (4.41)	0.32 (1.48)		−0.29 (−2.45)		0.35	3.05
$\Delta lnES$	1.02 (8.31)	0.16 (1.41)		−0.18 (−2.40)		0.35	3.06
ΔECS	0.82 (6.16)	0.12 (0.85)		0.09 (1.15)		0.21	1.49
$\Delta lnECS$	0.88 (11.35)	0.06 (0.74)		0.06 (1.14)		0.23	1.50
ΔECS	0.92 (6.68)		0.24 (1.49)		−0.13 (−1.58)	0.21	1.57
$\Delta lnECS$	0.96 (12.34)		0.13 (1.51)		−0.09 (−1.63)	0.25	1.61
ΔESS	1.14 (3.32)	0.30 (0.96)		−0.41 (−2.98)		0.42	3.11
$\Delta lnESS$	1.12 (5.58)	0.17 (0.93)		−0.28 (−2.89)		0.39	3.18
ΔESS	1.26 (3.46)		0.17 (0.52)	−0.40 (−2.82)		0.40	3.11
$\Delta lnESS$	1.20 (5.63)		0.08 (0.41)	−0.28 (−2.74)		0.39	3.17

Notes: All regressions shown are either linear or double-log forms, as indicated by the form of the dependent variable.

ΔEG^*	= increase in employment in the goods* sector between t-1 and t. Similarly for ΔES, etc.
$\Delta(ln)EG^*$	= increase in the log of employment in goods* between t-1 and t. Similarly for $\Delta lnES$, etc.
$\Delta(ln)Z$	= increase in (the log of) per capita GDP between t-1 and t.
$\Delta(ln)Z_{-1}$	= increase in (the log of) per capita GDP between t-2 and t-1. Similarly for $\Delta(ln)W_i$ and $\Delta(ln)W_{i,-1}$

For further notes see notes to Appendix Table A3.1.

Notes

2 Patterns of Structural Change and the Growth of Services

1. In (2.15)

$$\Pi = \begin{bmatrix} 1 - 3g + d_2 f^3 & -3d_2 b_1 f^2 & 3d_2 b_1^2 f & -d_2 b_1^3 \\ -d_2 f^3 & 3d_2 b_1 f^2 - 3d_2 b_1^2 f & d_2 b_1^3 \end{bmatrix}$$

2. Data for Brazil (1970) and Peru (1970) were omitted because earlier regressions indicated they diverge strongly from the pattern of other LDCs. Their inclusion does not significantly alter the comparisons in Table 2.1. Also data on economically active population rather than employment were used because although they may include varying amounts of unemployment, this effect is likely to be small and allows a larger sample of LDCs to be used.
3. By comparing coefficients in regressions (i), (ii) and (iii) with those in the Π matrix in note 1, it can be seen that sign predictions are satisfied.
4. Running OLS regressions on Fuchs (1968) data, using functional forms in (2.13) and (2.14) gives R^2s of 0.72 and 0.63 for Industry and Services respectively. ((2.14) expressed in terms of X becomes $y_1 = a - b(X - f)^3 - c/X$). This compares with Fuchs' results of 0.73 and 0.65 respectively (see Fuchs, 1968, p. 29n). Including data for the United States in 1960, changes in the R^2s respectively to 0.72 and 0.71, while adding the US observation to regressions of the functional forms used by Fuchs gives $R^2 = 0.65$ for Industry and $R^2 = 0.61$ for Services. Thus, with the inclusion of the US data, the functional forms of (2.13) and (2.14) give unambiguously improved results, even from this limited sample.
5. Where 1978 data were not available the nearest available year was used (usually 1977 or 1979). In the case of Sudan (where data are for 1956 and 1973) and Iraq (where data are for 1957 and 1977) it was assumed that structural changes took place evenly over the whole period, and only the latter half of the period was used to maximise comparability with other countries in the sample.

4 Economic Growth and Income Tax Revenue

1. An excellent comparative study of OECD country tax systems has recently been produced by Cnossen (1983).
2. Alternative approaches have been proposed by Spahn (1975) for the West German tax system, and by Hutton and Lambert (1980, 1980a) for the UK.

3. For 1977/78 values (using the middle of each income range as the y value, with £30,000 as the maximum mid-point), the following result was obtained using data from Meade (1978):

$$z = \begin{array}{cc} 1.05 & - \ 0.71x \ R^2 = 0.997, \ k = 0.5 \\ (112.44) & (-50.32) \end{array}$$

Figures in parentheses are t-values. This gives an asymptote of 1.05 and a 'standard rate' of 0.34 ($\beta = d - t_1$), and provides a very good fit. Slightly different values of d and k were used for the schedule of Figure 4.1 as the line was not constrained to go through the midpoints of the ranges.

4. The analytics are given in Creedy and Gemmell (1982, pp. 363–4).

5 Economic Growth and Revenue from a Tax/Transfer System

1. Some aspects of the tax advantages of contracting-out are discussed in Creedy and Gemmell (1984).
2. This is the system which operated in the UK prior to the small changes in the rate structure initiated in the 1985 Budget.
3. In fact the adjustment of the $r(q)$ relationship produces only a small effect on the built-in flexibility of VAT revenue, compared to a non-adjusting $r(q)$ relationship.
4. For example, the legislation requires that the NI upper earnings limit is approximately 7 times the lower limit, and that the former is about $1\frac{1}{2}$ times average earnings. Other values have been set accordingly.
5. A lognormal income distribution is again used here. Thus if the mean and variance of the logarithms are μ and σ^2 respectively, a set of values of y_i ($i = 1 \ldots N$) may be obtained using a set of random Normal deviates, u_i ($i = 1 \ldots N$). Experiments with different sample sizes showed that a sample size of 1000 is more than adequate for present purposes, in order to avoid significant sampling variation.
6. The upward or downward flexibility in total transfers reflects the ability of increases in the burden of income tax and NI faced by the low paid to be compensated by increases in the value of benefits. Simulations in which a_1 and a_2 were *not* indexed indicated that significant downward or upward flexibility in $T/\bar{y}$ can occur, depending on the level of mean income and the rate of *real* earnings growth. For example, at low rates of real earnings growth, $T/\bar{y}$ was found to fall sharply at low values of $\bar{y}$, but rise thereafter. This rise in $T/\bar{y}$ only occurs at low rates of real earnings growth because in this case more individuals continue to be in receipt of benefits, as average income rises.

6 Evidence from African, Asian and Latin American Studies

1. Bhalla equated 'modern' and 'traditional' services with those which are 'demand-induced' and 'supply-induced' respectively. Subsequent research (such as ILO, 1972) has shown that traditional services should not be

regarded as simply 'supply-induced' – i.e. arising out of an excess supply of labour.

2. In Philippines, Bhalla records a decline in employment in such modern services as hotels and lodging houses but a large rise in 'laundering, cleaning and dyeing'.

3. In 1976 only Israel had a larger employment share in services than Singapore's 61 per cent.

7 Structural Change and Employment Growth: Egypt, 1960–75

1. Disagreement and indecision towards the end of the First Five-Year Plan (1960–65) concerning the form and content of the new plan, meant the late introduction in 1966 of a plan to run to 1972, instead of a 1965–70 plan as originally intended. A ten-year plan was introduced in 1972.

2. Some recent evidence on the 1970–79 period by Hansen and Radwan (1982) suggests that some of the service sector employment expansion, identified in this chapter up to 1975, has continued particularly in government services. However they also suggest that higher demand for labour in the later 1970s has probably reduced the growth of private, informal services. See Hansen and Radwan (1982, pp. 535–541).

3. See Fisher (1939), Clark (1940), Chenery (1960), Maizels (1963) and Thirlwall (1972).

4. See, for example, Beck (1979, 1982).

8 Influences on Service Employment Growth in Egypt

1. The commonly-used time trend to model technology effects is highly unsatisfactory, not least because of the implied assumption that technology improvements occur in a smooth and uniform manner. Many empirical studies find time trends highly significant in their results and it is likely that it is a proxy for many factors other than technology.

2. A difference equation in logs, whereby $\Delta lnE_i = f\ (\Delta lnZ,\ \Delta lnW_i)$ is, of course, equivalent to examining the relationship between the proportionate growth rates of Z and W_i and the rate of employment growth.

3. The inclusion of productivity (as measured by output per man) *and* output variables in an employment function raises particular econometric difficulties because of the identity linking the three variables.

4. Obviously the two variables are not statistically independent since they share a common term – output. However it must be assumed that there are no causal relationships between the variables in terms of economic behaviour.

5. Although the prices of many services probably did increase by less than those of many goods in this period, the difference implicit in real GDP data almost certainly exaggerates this and the assumption of equal price rises across sectors is probably closer to the truth. For a discussion of price deflator problems in Egypt, see Kanovsky (1970, p. 219).

6.   Of course not all of the urban population increase represents increases in
      the labour force. However Egypt's population has been growing rapidly
      since the Second World War, causing a very large number of entrants into
      the labour force over this period resulting from earlier increases in
      population.
7.   The public/private breakdown of GDP data 1960–5 and 1974 are from
      different sources and therefore may not be strictly comparable.
8.   Alternative measures of social service sector expenditure (including or
      excluding local and investment expenditures) all suggest a rise relative to
      GDP from 1960–5 but subsequent falls to 1970 and 1975. Some effects of
      such a rise are examined in Chapter 9.
9.   Movements in these relative prices between goods and services can in fact
      be deduced from the data in Tables 8.6, 8.7 and 8.9. It can be shown that if
      $(\dot{Q}_s - \dot{Q}_g)_{\mathrm{I}} > (\dot{Q}_s - \dot{Q}_g)_{\mathrm{II}}$ then goods sector price increases exceed service
      sector price increases.

9   The Role of the Non-market Sector in Egypt

1.   The required productivity increase will also be influenced by the way in
      which the market to non-market transfer is financed. Taxation-financed
      expenditure for example can be expected to produce different effects on
      demand from expenditure financed by government borrowing from the
      bank or non-bank sectors.
2.   A rise in the ratio of household saving to personal disposable income in
      the UK and Greece has been put forward by Bacon and Karayinnis-
      Bacon as one explanation of a falling value of c_m in both countries. It is
      difficult to establish if this has been important in Egypt, since data are not
      available on household saving, but a crude ratio of total saving to total
      disposable income shows no tendency to rise when c_m is falling. Only if
      household saving increased significantly at the expense of corporate
      saying, would such an explanation be plausible in this case.
3.   This is the weighted average of actual rates achieved using definition (1) in
      Table 3, namely 4.2 per cent for non-market employment and 2.7 per cent
      for market sector employment. If the market sector is more capital
      intensive than the non-market sector, equalising $\dot{G}_m$ and $\dot{C}_m$ may not
      equalise employment growth rates.
4.   The composition of the wholesale price index in Egypt is considered, by
      some commentators, to be a more accurate calculation of how prices
      actually change than the 'cost of living' index, and has therefore been
      preferred here. See el Kammash (1968, p. 154).

References

ABDEL-FADIL, M. (1975). *Development, Income Distribution and Social Change in Egypt 1952–70* (Cambridge University Press).

ABDEL-FADIL, M. (1980). *The Political Economy of Nasserism* (Cambridge University Press).

ABIZADEH, S. and WYCKOFF, J. B. (1982). 'Tax system components and economic development: An international perspective', *Bulletin for International Fiscal Documentation*, 36, 483–491.

AITCHISON, J. A. and BROWN, J. A. C. (1957). *The Lognormal Distribution* (Cambridge University Press).

BACON, R. W. and ELTIS, W. A. (1976). *Britain's Economic Problem: Two Few Producers* (London: Macmillan) (2nd Edition, 1978).

BACON, R. W. and KARAYIANNIS-BACON, H. (1980). 'The growth of the non-market sector in a newly industrialised country: The case of Greece', *Greek Economic Review*, 2, 44–64.

BAUMOL, W. J. (1967). 'The Macroeconomics of Unbalanced Growth', *American Economic Review*, 57, 415–26.

BAUER, P. T. and YAMEY, B. S. (1957). *The Economics of Underdeveloped Countries* (Cambridge University Press).

BECK, M. (1979). 'Public sector growth: A real perspective', *Public Finance*, 34, 313–56.

BECK, M. (1982). 'Toward a theory of public sector growth', *Public Finance*, 37, 163–77.

BELL, D. (1974). *The Coming of Post-Industrial Society* (London: Heinemann Educational Books).

BERGER, M. (1954). *Bureaucracy and Society in Modern Egypt* (New York: Praeger).

BERLINCK, M. T., BOVO, J. M. and CINTRA, L. C. (1981). 'The urban informal sector and industrial development in a small city: The case of Campinas'. In S. V. Sethuraman (ed.), *The Urban Informal Sector in Developing Countries. Employment, Poverty and Environment* (Geneva: ILO).

BERRY, A. (1978). 'A positive interpretation of the expansion of urban services in Latin America with some Colombian evidence', *Journal of Development Studies*, 14, 210–31.

BHAGWATI, J. N. (1984). 'Why are services cheaper in the poor countries?', *Economic Journal*, 94, 279–86.

BHALLA, A. S. (1970). 'The role of services in employment expansion', *International Labour Review*, 101, 519–39.

BHALLA, A. S. (1973). 'A disaggregative approach to LDCs tertiary sector', *International Labour Review*, 101, 519–39.

BIRD, R. M. (1971). 'Wagner's Law of expanding state activity', *Public Finance*, 26, 1–26.

BLACKABY, F. (ed.) (1978). *De-Industrialisation* (London: Heinemann Educational Books/NIESR).

BLADES, D., JOHNSTON, D. D., and MARCZEWSKI, W. (1974). *Service Activities in Developing Countries* (Paris, OECD).

205

BROMLEY, R. (1978). 'Organisation, regulation and exploitation in the so-called 'urban informal sector': The street traders of Cali, Colombia', *World Development*, 6, 1161–71.

BROWN, C. J. F. and SHERIFF, T. D. (1978). 'De-Industrialisation: A Background Paper', in Blackaby, F. (ed.) *De-Industrialisation* (London; Heinemann Educational Books/NIESR).

CHENERY, H. B. (1960). 'Patterns of industrial growth', *American Economic Review*, 50, 624–654.

CHENERY, H. B. (1979). *Structural Change and Development Policy* (Oxford University Press for World Bank).

CHENERY, H. B. and TAYLOR, L. (1968). 'Development patterns: Among countries and over time', *Review of Economics and Statistics*, 50, 391–416.

CHENERY, H. B. and SYRQUIN, M. (1975). *Patterns of Development 1950–70* (Oxford University Press for World Bank).

CHRYSTAL, K. A. (1983). *Controversies in Macroeconomics* Oxford: Philip Allan), 2nd Edition.

CLARK, C. (1940). *The Conditions of Economic Progress* (London: Macmillan).

CNOSSEN, C. (1983). *Comparative Tax Studies. Essays in Honor of Richard Goode* (Amsterdam: North-Holland).

CREEDY, J. and GEMMELL, N. (1982). 'The built-in flexibility of progressive income taxes: A simple model', *Public Finance*, 37, 361–71.

CREEDY, J. and GEMMELL, N. (1984). 'Income redistribution through taxes and transfers in Britain', *Scottish Journal of Political Economy*, 31, 44–59.

CREEDY, J. and GEMMELL, N. (1985). 'The indexation of taxes and transfers in Britain', *Manchester School*, 53, 364–84.

DORRINGTON, J. C. (1974). 'A structural approach to estimating the built-in flexibility of United Kingdom taxes on personal income', *Economic Journal*, 84, 576–94.

ECONOMIST INTELLIGENCE UNIT (EIU) (1967). 'Egypt. The Economy', *Quarterly Economic Review. Egypt (UAR), Libya, Sudan*, 1 (March), 7–11.

ENGELS, F. (1892). *The Conditions of the Working-Class in England in 1844* (London: George Allen & Unwin edition, 1920).

FABRICANT, S. (1952). *The Trend of Government Activity in the United States Since 1900* (New York: NBER).

FAPOHUNDA, O. J. (1981). 'Human resources and the Lagos informal sector'. In S. V. Sethuraman (ed.), *The Urban Informal Sector in Developing Countries. Employment, Poverty and Environment* (Geneva: ILO).

FIELDS, G. S. (1975). 'Rural-urban migration, urban unemployment and underemployment and job-search activity in LDCs', *Journal of Development Economics*, 2, 165–187.

FISHER, A. G. B. (1933). 'Capital and the growth of knowledge', *Economic Journal*, 43, 379–89.

FISHER, A. G. B. (1939). 'Production: primary, secondary and tertiary', *Economic Record*, 15, 24–38.

FOWLER, D. A. (1981). 'The informal sector in Freetown: Opportunities for self-employment'. In S. V. Sethuraman (ed.), *The Urban Informal Sector in Developing Countries. Employment, Poverty and Environment* (Geneva: ILO).

FUCHS, V. (1965). *The Growing Importance of the Service Industries* (New York: NBER, Occasional Paper, 96).

FUCHS, V. (1968). *The Service Economy* (New York: NBER).

GEMMELL, N. (1982). 'The role of the non-market sector in Egypt's economic growth, 1960–76', *Oxford Economic Papers*, 34, 207–23.

GEMMELL, N. (1982a). 'Economic development and structural change: The role of the service sector', *Journal of Development Studies*, 19, 37–66.

GEMMELL, N. (1983). 'International comparisons of the effects of non-market sector growth', *Journal of Comparative Economics*, 7, 368–81.

GEMMELL, N. (1985). 'The growth of employment in services: Egypt, 1960–75', *The Developing Economies*, 23, 53–68.

GERSHUNY, J. I. (1977). 'Post-industrial society: The myth of the service economy', *Futures*, 9, 103–14.

GERSHUNY, J. I. (1978). *After Industrial Society* (London: Macmillan).

HANAFI, M. and MONGI, M. (1975). *Labour Absorption in the Egyptian Economy* (Cairo: Institute of National Planning).

HANSEN, B. and RADWAN, S. (1982). 'Employment planning in Egypt: An insurance for the future', *International Labour Review*, 121, 535–51.

HART, K. (1973). 'Informal income opportunities and urban employment in Ghana', *Journal of Modern African Studies*, 11, 61–89.

HINRICHS, H. H. (1965). 'Determinants of government revenue shares among less developed countries', *Economic Journal*, 75, 546–56.

HINRICHS, H. H. (1966). *A General Theory of Tax Structure Change During Economic Development* (Cambridge: Law School of Harvard University).

HUTTON, J. P. and LAMBERT, P. J. (1980). 'Evaluating income tax revenue elasticities', *Economic Journal*, 90, 901–6.

HUTTON, J. P. and LAMBERT, P. J. (1980a). *Income tax, inflation tax and the tax elasticity: A model for the UK*, Institute of Social and Economic Research, University of York, Department of Economics and Related Studies Discussion Paper No. 59.

HUTTON, J. P. and LAMBERT, P. J. (1982). 'Modelling the effects of income growth and discretionary change on the sensitivity of UK income tax revenue', *Economic Journal*, 92, 145–55.

IKRAM, K. (1980). *Egypt: Economic Management in a Period of Transition* (Oxford University Press for World Bank).

INTERNATIONAL LABOUR OFFICE (ILO) (1972). *Employment, Incomes and Equality: A Strategy for Increasing Productive Employment in Kenya* (Geneva: ILO).

ISSAWI, C. (1961). 'Egypt since 1800; a study of lop-sided development', *Journal of Economic History*, 21, 1–25.

JOHNSTON, J. (1975). 'A macro model of inflation', *Economic Journal*, 85, 288–308.

JURADO, G. M. *et al.* (1981). 'The Manila informal sector: In transition?'. In S. V. Sethuraman (ed.), *The Urban Informal Sector in Developing Countries. Employment, Poverty and Environment* (Geneva: ILO).

KALDOR, N. (1966). *Causes of the Slow Rate of Growth of the United Kingdom*. Inaugural Lecture (Cambridge University Press).

KAMMASH, M. N. EL- (1968). *Economic Development and Planning in Egypt* (New York: Praeger).

KANOVSKY, E. (1970). *The Economy Impact of the Six-Days War* (New York: Praeger).

KATOUSIAN, M. A. (1970). 'The development of the service sector: A new approach', *Oxford Economic Papers*, 22, 362–82.

KAY, J. and KING, M. A. (1980). *The British Tax System* (Oxford University Press).

KRAVIS, I. B., KENNESAY, Z., HESTON, A., and SUMMERS, R. (1975). *A System of International Comparisons of Gross Product and Purchasing Power* (Johns Hopkins University Press).

KRAVIS, I. B., HESTON, A., and SUMMERS, R. (1978). 'Real GDP per capita for more than one hundred countries', *Economic Journal*, 88, 215–42.

KRAVIS, I. B., HESTON, A., and SUMMERS, R. (1982). 'The share of services in economic growth'. In F. G. Adams and B. Hickman (eds.), *Global Econometrics: Essays in Honor of Lawrence R. Klein* (Cambridge: MIT Press).

KUZNETS, S. (1957). 'Quantitative aspects of the economic growth of nations: II Industrial distribution of national product and labour force', *Economic Development and Cultural Change*, 5 (No. 4: Supplement), 3–111.

KUZNETS, S. (1966). *Modern Economic Growth* (New Haven: Yale University Press).

LEWIS, W. A. (1954). 'Economic development with unlimited supplies of labour', *Manchester School*, 22, 139–91.

LEWIS, W. A. (1978). *The Evolution of the International Economic Order* (Princeton University Press).

MABRO, R. (1974). *The Egyptian Economy* (Oxford: Clarendon Press).

MABRO, R. and O'BRIEN, P. K. (1970). 'Structural changes in the Egyptian economy 1937–1965', in M. A. Cook (ed.), *Studies in the Economic History of the Middle-East* (Oxford University Press).

MABRO, R. and RADWAN, S. *The Industrialisation of Egypt, 1939–1973* (Oxford: Clarendon Press).

MAIZELS, A. (1963). *Industrial Growth and World Trade* (Cambridge Univeristy Press for NIESR).

MAJUMDAR, A. (1980). *In-migration and the Informal Sector* (New Delhi: Vision Books).

MARGA INSTITUTE, COLOMBO (1981). 'Informal sector without migration: The case of Colombo'. In S. V. Sethuraman (ed.), *The Urban Informal Sector in Developing Countries. Employment, Poverty and Environment* (Geneva: ILO).

MARTIN, A. and LEWIS, W. A. (1956). 'Patterns of public revenue and expenditure', *Manchester School*, 24, 203–44.

MAZUMDAR, D. (1973). *The Theory of Urban Underemployment in Less Developed Countries* (Washington: World Bank, mimeo).

MEAD, D. C. (1967). *Growth and Structural Change in the Egyptian Economy* (Homewood, Illinois: Richard D. Irwin).

MEAD, D. C. (1982). 'Small industries in Egypt: An exploration of the economics of small-scale furniture producers', *International Journal of Middle-East Studies*, 14, 159–71.

MEADE, J. E. (1978). *The Structure and Reform of Direct Taxation* (London: George Allen and Unwin).

MERRICK, R. W. (1976). 'Employment and earnings in the informal sector in Brazil: The case of Belo Horizonte', *Journal of Developing Areas*, 10, 337–54.

MESSERE, K. (1983). 'Trends in OECD tax revenues'. In S. Cnossen (ed.), *Comparative Tax Studies. Essays in Honor of Richard Goode* (Amsterdam: North-Holland).

MOIR, H. (1981). 'Occupational mobility and the informal sector in Jakarta'. In S. V. Sethuraman (ed.), *The Urban Informal Sector in Developing Countries. Employment, Poverty and Environment* (Geneva: ILO).

MOSER, C. O. N. (1977). 'The dual economy and marginality debate and the contribution of micro analysis: Market sellers in Bogota', *Development and Change*, 8, 465–89.

MOSER, C. O. N. (1978). 'Informal sector or petty commodity production: Dualism or dependence in urban development?', *World Development*, 6, 1041–64.

MUSGRAVE, R. A. (1969). *Fiscal Systems* (New Haven: Yale University Press).

NIHAN, G., DEMOL, E., and JONDOH, C. (1979). 'The modern informal sector in Lomé', *International Labour Review*, 118, 631–44.

NISKANEN, W. A. (1971). *Bureaucracy and Representative Government* (Chicago: Aldine Atherton).

OECD (1975). *Adjustment for Trade* (Paris: Development Centre, OECD).

OFER, G. (1967). *Service Industries in Israel* (New York: Praeger).

OWEN, E. R. J. (1969). *Cotton in the Egyptian Economy* (Oxford University Press).

PEACOCK, A. T. and WISEMAN, J. (1961). *The Growth of Public Expenditure in the United Kingdom* (Princeton University Press).

RADWAN, S. (1974). *Capital Formation in Egyptian Industry and Agriculture, 1882–1967* (London: Ithaca Press).

RADWAN, S. (1977). *The Impact of Agrarian Reform on Rural Egypt (1952–75)* (Geneva: ILO, World Employment Programme Research Working Paper 13).

SANCHEZ, C. F., PALMIERO, H., and FERRERO, F. (1981). 'The informal and quasi-formal sectors in Cordoba'. In S. V. Sethuraman (ed.), *The Urban Informal Sector in Developing Countries. Employment, Poverty and Environment* (Geneva: ILO).

SEOW, G. F. H. (1979). 'The service sector in Singapore's economy: Performance and structure', *Malayan Economic Review*, 24, 46–73.

SETHURAMAN, S. V. (1981). *The Urban Informal Sector in Developing Countries. Employment, Poverty and Environment* (Geneva: ILO).

SINHA, J. N. (1968). 'Employment in trade–the Indian experience', *Indian Economic Journal*, 16, 53–67.

SMITH, A (1976). *An Inquiry into the Nature and Causes of the Wealth of Nations*, Edited (by Andrew Skinner) and reprinted as *The Wealth of Nations* (Harmondsworth: Penguin Books, 1970).

SPAHN, P. B. (1975). 'Simulating long-term changes of income distribution within an income tax model for West Germany', *Public Finance*, 30, 231–50.

STIGLER, G. L. (1956). *Trends in Employment in the Service Industries* (Princeton University Press).

THORBECKE, E. (1973). 'The employment problem: A critical evaluation of four ILO comprehensive county reports', *International Labour Review*, 107, 393–423.

THIRLWALL, A. P. (1972). *Growth and Development* (London: Macmillan) (2nd Edition, 1978).

THIRLWALL, A. P. (1982). 'Deindustrialisation in the United Kingdom', *Lloyds Bank Review*, 144, 22–37.

TURNHAM, D. (1971). *The Employment Problem in Less Developed Countries* (Paris: OECD).

UN ECONOMIC COMMISSION FOR EUROPE (1977). *Structure and Change in European Industry* (New York: UN).

WAGNER, A. (1883). Translated and Reprinted as, 'Three extracts on public finance' in R. A. Musgrave and A. T. Peacock (eds.) *Classics in the Theory of Public Finance* (London: Macmillan, 1962).

WEEKS, J. (1975). 'Policies for expanding employment in the informal sector of developing countries', *International Labour Review*, 111, 1–13.

WILLIAMSON, J. G. (1961). 'Public expenditure and revenue: An international comparison', *Manchester School*, 29, 34–56.

Author Index

211

Subject Index